Poems of

ANNE BRADSTREET

Poems of
ANNE BRADSTREET

Edited with an Introduction by
ROBERT HUTCHINSON

DOVER PUBLICATIONS, INC.
New York

Published in Canada by General Publishing Company, Ltd.,
30 Lesmill Road, Don Mills, Toronto, Ontario.
Published in the United Kingdom by Constable and Company, Ltd.,
10 Orange Street, London W.C.2.

Poems of Anne Bradstreet is a new collection, published
for the first time by Dover Publications, Inc., in 1969. Full
bibliographical information on the source of the text is to
be found on page 35.

Standard Book Number: 486-22160-1
Library of Congress Catalog Card Number: 77-76985

Manufactured in the United States of America

DOVER PUBLICATIONS, INC.
180 Varick Street
New York, N.Y. 10014

CONTENTS

Introduction   1
A Note on the Text   35

PART ONE: SHORTER POEMS

The Author to her Book   40

I / *Love Poems*

To my Dear and loving Husband   41
"As loving Hind"   41
"Phœbus make haste"   42
A Letter to her Husband, absent upon Publick
    employment   44
Before the Birth of one of her Children   45

II / *Domestic Poems*

In reference to her Children, 23. June, 1656   47
Upon a Fit of Sickness, Anno. 1632. Ætatis suæ, 19   50
To her Father with some verses   51
To the Memory of my dear and ever honoured
    Father Thomas Dudley Esq; Who deceased,
    July 31. 1653. and of his Age, 77   51
An Epitaph On my dear and ever honoured
    Mother Mrs. Dorothy Dudley, who deceased
    Decemb. 27. 1643. and of her age, 61   54
Upon the burning of our house, July 10th, 1666   54
Upon some distemper of body   56
In memory of my dear grand-child Elizabeth
    Bradstreet, who deceased August, 1665. being
    a year and a half old   57
In memory of my dear grand-child Anne Brad-
    street. Who deceased June 20. 1669. being
    three years and seven Moneths old   57

On my dear Grand-child Simon Bradstreet, Who dyed on 16. Novemb. 1669. being but a moneth, and one day old 58

To the memory of my dear Daughter in Law, Mrs. Mercy Bradstreet, who deceased Sept. 6. 1669. in the 28. year of her Age 58

III | *Religious Meditations*

To my Dear Children 61

"By night when others soundly slept" 61

For Deliverance from a feaver 62

From another sore Fitt 63

Deliverance from a fitt of Fainting 64

"What God is like to him I serve" 65

"My soul, rejoice thou in thy God" 66

"As spring the winter doth succeed" 67

Upon my Son Samuel his goeing for England, Novem. 6, 1657 68

"My thankfull heart with glorying Tongue" 68

For the restoration of my dear Husband from a burning Ague, June, 1661 69

Upon my Daughter Hannah Wiggin her recovery from a dangerous feaver 70

On my Sons Return out of England, July 17, 1661 70

Upon my dear and loving husband his goeing into England, Jan. 16, 1661 72

In my Solitary houres in my dear husband his Absence 74

In thankfull acknowledgment for the letters I received from my husband out of England 76

In thankfull Remembrance for my dear husbands safe Arrivall Sept. 3, 1662 76

"As weary pilgrim, now at rest" 77

IV | *Contemplations*   79

V | *Dialogues and Lamentations*

The Flesh and the Spirit   89
The Vanity of all worldly things   92
Davids Lamentation for Saul and Jonathan   94
A Dialogue between Old England and New;
     concerning their present Troubles, Anno, 1642   95

VI | *Formal Elegies*

In Honour of that High and Mighty Princess
     Queen Elizabeth of happy memory   105
An Elegie upon that Honourable and renowned
     Knight Sir Philip Sidney, who was untimely
     slain at the Siege of Zutphen, Anno, 1586   109
In honour of Du Bartas, 1641   112

PART TWO: LONGER POEMS

To her most Honoured Father Thomas Dudley
     Esq; these humbly presented   117
The Prologue [to *The Tenth Muse*]   118
The Four Elements   120
     Fire   121
     Earth   124
     Water   128
     Air   132
Of the four Humours in Mans Constitution   135
     Choler   136
     Blood   140
     Melancholy   145
     Flegme   149
Of the four Ages of Man   153
     Childhood   155
     Youth   157

    Middle Age   160

    Old Age   163

The four Seasons of the Year   167

    Spring   167

    Summer   169

    Autumn   172

    Winter   174

The four Monarchyes, the Assyrian being the first, beginning under Nimrod, 131. Years after the Flood   175

    Belshazzar   176

    An Apology   177

Appendix A. Autobiographical Passages in the Bradstreet Manuscript   179

Appendix B. Meditations Divine and morall (selection)   187

Notes   195

Selected Bibliography   215

Index of Titles and First Lines   219

INTRODUCTION

In 1630, Anne Dudley Bradstreet was a passenger aboard John Winthrop's flagship *Arbella* as it moved out of Southampton Waters to lead three other ships toward the New World. With her were her parents, Thomas and Dorothy Dudley, and her young husband, Simon Bradstreet. Under Winthrop's direction twelve heads of families, including Anne Bradstreet's father, had banded at Cambridge, England, the summer before; there they had agreed to found the Massachusetts Bay Colony, promising to take their families to America, where their more zealous cousins the Pilgrims had settled ten years earlier. Mrs. Bradstreet was eighteen, two years married, delicate, her face probably still marked from the smallpox she had suffered the year of her marriage. Few seeing her at her husband's side helping to arrange their few possessions on deck would have thought she could survive a New England winter, much less carry on the hard duties of a magistrate's wife, give birth to eight healthy children, and write a book that would be the sensation of its own age and one of the delights of ours.

The churning of the crowded vessel and the strange New World it must have symbolized were a marked contrast to the life she had known before, on the vast estates of the Earl of Lincoln in the low, flat, marshy Lincolnshire country in the east of England. Her father, who once fought for Queen Elizabeth against Philip II and was perhaps present at the siege of Amiens in 1597, had, upon completion of his military duties, been recommended to the young Earl as chief steward, and had patiently for a dozen years cleared the estates of their debts. The position was a boon to his growing family—five children by 1621—but to none more than his second child and eldest daughter, Anne, who besides loving nature and the fens and canals of the countryside, enjoyed books and ideas, and came to know in the Earl's large library in his Castle of Sempringham some of the modern writers of the day: Spenser, Sidney, Archbishop Usher and Dr. Crooke, and Drayton, Browne, Wither, Sylvester and du Bartas—a hoard of knowledge that would later surprise her American neighbors. She was a very well-read girl by the time she married her father's twenty-five-year-old assistant on the estate, the man who was to be her companion for life: Simon Bradstreet, nine years older than herself, a graduate of Emmanuel College, Cambridge, who in the New World would become eventually Governor of Massachusetts, legislator, judge, ambassador, and royal councillor, dying in great honor at ninety-four.

If the times had been different, one might have predicted an idyllic life for the young couple on the Earl of Lincoln's estate. But England was torn by religious dissension and suspicion; the strict measures of the tragic Archbishop Laud and the flames of civil war lay only a few years ahead, and already there was much that seemed threatening in the acts of Archbishop Bancroft. Nonconformist ministers were silenced, driven into exile; people expressed their real thoughts, if at all, in whispers. It was unfortunate for Anne Bradstreet that her father, at this inappropriate time, heard the preaching of the Puritan ministers Dodd and Hildersham and was converted for life to Nonconformism. It was not a strict kind of Puritanism—not like that of the Pilgrims, which demanded complete separation from the Anglican Church—and had circumstances been different he could have continued indefinitely in the employ of the Earl of Lincoln, who had Puritan tendencies himself. The death in 1625 of James I and the accession of Charles I to the throne put an end to such hopes. Charles failed to repudiate the growing authority of Laud, already bishop of London; he called two Parliaments and in a bitter struggle dissolved them both. When in March, 1629, he dissolved the second session of his third Parliament, it seemed to Winthrop, Dudley, and members of what would later be called "the great migration" a deciding moment. The New World would shelter them, as it had the group at Plymouth Plantation. Advance parties had already been sent out to Salem and Charlestown. It would be easier, hundreds of miles away and with an ocean between, to maintain their position as loyal dissenters. About their loyalty there was no doubt: they went as sons of England, not as rebels, and their city in the "savage deserts of America" would be a model not of separatism but of justice—a "city set on a hill."

Winthrop wrote, "I shall call that my country where I may most glorify God and enjoy the presence of my dearest friends."

The colonists' first glimpse of the new country, after seventy-two sickness-filled days aboard the *Arbella*, was hardly reassuring. Physically it was beautiful: the season was May, all was in bloom, wild strawberries were growing almost at high-tide mark. Winthrop noted "the fine, fresh smell like a garden"—the smell of wild grape and corn-blossom. The group of advance colonists at Salem, however, showed that the winter had been a terrible one. "We found the Colony in a sad and unexpected condition," wrote Anne's father, "above eight of them being dead the winter before; and many of those alive, weak and sick. . . . We found ourselves wholly unable to feed them." The group at Charlestown seemed nearly as desperate, with a water supply consisting of "a brackish spring in sands by the water side." The families from the *Arbella*, many of them sick of the scurvy, wondered where the Lord had brought them. Anne Bradstreet in her writing never directly referred to the hardships of the voyage, but the near-despair is still present in the lines she wrote thirty years later:

> Remember, Lord, thy folk, whom thou
> To wildernesse hast brought.

They may have lived, those first few months, in wigwams or dugout houses cut out of the hillside.

Cambridge was at last settled upon as the most desirable community, and the small group of colonists spent their first winter there, the Bradstreets building their house at "Brayntree" and Wood Streets, which later generations would call Harvard Square. Although they were among the richest families of the party, wealth meant little that first winter, when they had, as her father wrote, "no table, nor other room to write in than by the fireside upon my knee," and had little to eat, living often upon "clams and museles and ground nuts and acorns."

In two often-quoted sentences in the small manuscript book she wrote for her children, reprinted in part in Appendix A (p. 179), Anne Bradstreet recorded her disillusionment and rebellion at the new life which awaited them.

> After a short time I changed my condition and was marryed, and came into this Country, where I found a new world and new manners, at which my heart rose.

But because she was a Puritan, she could resolve the rebellious rising of her heart in acquiescence to the divine will:

> But after I was convinced it was the way of God, I submitted to it and joined the church at Boston.

She had had similar periods of rebelliousness, she wrote, as a young girl, in spite of her dedication to goodness at an early age:

> In my young years, about 6 or 7 as I take it, I began to make conscience of my wayes, and what I knew was sinfull, as lying, disobedience to Parents, &c. I avoided it . . . I could not be at rest 'till by prayer I had confest it unto God. . . . I also found much comfort in reading the Scriptures. . . .

But at fourteen and fifteen

> I found my heart more carnall, and sitting loose from God.

It took the shock of smallpox, in the year of her marriage to Simon Bradstreet, to humble her heart:

> When I was in my affliction, I besought the Lord, and confessed my Pride and Vanity and he was entreated of me, and again restored me.

Now she was perplexed with an even more trying problem: she did not understand why she had not yet had a child:

> It pleased God to keep me a long time without a child, which was a great greif to me, and cost mee many prayers and tears before I obtain one.

In 1633, however, her first child, a son, Samuel, was born, and after him were to come "many more, of whom I now take the care." A second child, Dorothy, was born in 1634, at about the time Anne Bradstreet fell into a "lingering sicknes like a consumption, together with a lamenesse, which correction I saw the Lord sent to humble and try me." The first poem we have of hers, written at the age of nineteen (p. 50), was about an illness, and she was to write many more on this subject. For all her seemingly high spirits, she was to suffer from a variety of sicknesses nearly all of her adult life.

In 1634 it was decided that the "land aboute Cochichowiske [Andover] shall be reserved for an island plantacon." This is the first mention in America of Andover, which was to be the Bradstreets' home for the remainder of their lives. By the time they moved there from Ipswich, a temporary home, two more children had been born—Sarah and Simon—and Anne's father, Thomas Dudley, had served not only as judge, Assistant Governor, and Deputy Governor, but, upon Winthrop's departure, as Governor of Massachusetts, a post Anne's husband Simon Bradstreet would also hold, but not until 1679, seven years after her death.

North Andover was to be their final and happiest home. One thinks of Anne in the large frame house close to the meeting house, standing before one of the huge open fireplaces characteristic of the period or crouching her way up dark, narrow, curving wooden staircases to gaze out the tiny lozenge-shaped windows for what could be seen of her glorious New England back yard. In this house were born the last four children—Hannah, Mercy, Dudley, and John—of the group of eight so charmingly presented in the poem beginning "I had eight birds hatcht in one nest" (p. 47).

It was in North Andover, too, that Anne learned of the death, in 1643, of her mother and, in 1653, of her father. She wrote poems in their honor, but not with the shattering pathos of the group of poems she wrote upon the deaths of her grandchildren Elizabeth Bradstreet, aged a year and a half (1665); Anne Bradstreet, aged three years and seven months (1669); Simon Bradstreet, "being but a moneth, and one day old" (1669); and of her daughter-in-law Mercy Bradstreet, wife of her son Samuel, who died in childbirth (pp. 57–59).

In North Andover (or by its old name, Merrimack) Anne took the kind of walks that she describes in her "Contemplations," and fulfilled, besides her ordinary household chores, the many duties of the wife of a busy public official. Like many another political figure's wife, she suffered much from being alone: many of her poems are prayers for the safety of her husband or letters to him while he was on some official mission. At one point both her eldest son Samuel, twenty at the time, and her husband were in England on separate enterprises, Samuel after his graduation from Harvard, her husband on much more important business. In the Restoration of 1660 Charles II had come to the throne, and the Massachusetts colonists, who had been indifferent to his cause during the Civil Wars, feared they might be punished as a result. Bradstreet and the Reverend John Norton, chosen to allay Charles's anger, returned with fair success, but not before rumors came that they had been shipwrecked, detained, or were even in the Tower.

In 1666 occurred the tragic fire referred to in the poem "Upon the burning of our house" (p. 54) and in the concluding verses of "The four Monarchyes." A careless maid apparently placed hot ashes in a hogshead over the porch of the Bradstreet house and burned the house to the ground. Her son wrote of the fire:

> I lost my Books, and many of my clothes, to the valeiu of 50 or 60 lb at least; the Lord gave, and the Lord hath taken, blessed bee the Name of the Lord.

The number of books destroyed was, he says, over 800, a sizable library in a country that had not had tables to write on only a few years before.

The house was rebuilt, but where it was and exactly how long Mrs. Bradstreet lived in it is not known. She was getting old, and suffering more and more from the disease that wracked her body. Her last poem, reproduced in her handwriting on pages 38 and 39, speaks longingly of heaven, and of her desire to find new life there:

> Lord make me ready for that day
> then Come deare bridgrome Come away.

When she died, in 1672, at the age of sixty, her son Simon records:

> Her death was occasioned by a consumption being wasted to skin & bone & She had an issue made in her arm bec' she was much troubled with rheum, & one of ye women y^t tended herr dressing her arm, s'd shee never saw such an arm in her Life, I, s'd my most dear Mother, but y^t arm shall bee a Glorious Arm.

All but one of her children, Dorothy, were living at the time of her death. Her next to youngest, Dudley, was for a time suspected in the witchcraft troubles, but survived this, along with imprisonment by the Indians. Anne Bradstreet had fifty-three grandchildren. Among her descendants were such eminent figures as Oliver Wendell Holmes, Richard Henry Dana, William Ellery Channing, and Charles Eliot Norton.

Her burial place is unknown. No stone bearing her name has been found, and no portrait has been discovered.

II

Such was the life of Anne Bradstreet, or would have been if in 1650 one of the most extraordinary events in English and American literature had not taken place—in that year was published, in London, at the Sign of the Bible in Popes Head-Alley, a book entitled *The Tenth Muse Lately sprung up in America. Or Severall Poems, compiled with great variety of Wit and Learning, full of delight. . . . By a Gentle-woman in those parts.* The title page carried no name, but the many commendatory verses (including the delightful one by Ipswich's uninhibited Nat Ward, reproduced here in the Notes, p. 208), testified to its authorship by an American woman, "Mistris *Anne Bradstreet*, Vertue's true and lively Patterne, Wife of the Worshipfull *Simon Bradstreet* Esquire. At present residing in the Occidentall parts of the World, in *America*, alias *NOV-ANGLIA*." A book by an American— and by an American woman! It was unthinkable. To some it might have seemed almost criminal.

A poet in America—how was that possible where there were no books, barely a university, where all one's energies were needed to clear forests and keep the savages at bay? And a woman—what woman would dare, when all her countrywomen were busy with their needlework, farming, and prayers? It was, after all, about that time, as Ann Stanford has reminded us, that Anne Hopkins, wife of the Governor of Hartford, was considered insane because she "wrote" and neglected her housework.

The questions soon gave way, in England at least, to more pressing ones: the year 1650, only months after Charles I had been beheaded at Whitehall and at the very time Oliver Cromwell was defeating the Presbyterian Scots at Dunbar, was hardly the most auspicious time for an American to publish a book of poems, even if they did reflect the shadows of those events. But to her American neighbors (as to readers of today) an explanation must have seemed necessary.

Was the woman, then, sane and respectable? Yes, according to the book's introduction (see Notes, p. 207), written apparently by her brother-in-law: she was "honoured, and esteemed where she lives, for her gracious demeanour, her eminent parts, her pious conversation." Nor had she stolen time from her housework to do it: these poems "are the fruit but of some few houres, curtailed from her sleep and other refreshments." She had not even given her consent for them to appear: "I fear the displeasure of no person," wrote her brother-in-law, "but the Author, without whose knowledg" the poems had been brought to public view.

The facts of publication are by now familiar. Mrs. Bradstreet's brother-in-law, the Reverend John Woodbridge of Andover, husband of her younger sister Mercy, returned to England for several years in 1647 and took with him the manuscript of *The Tenth Muse*, feeling that London's sixty printers could do better with it than New England's one (the fact that Herrick's *Hesperides* had just appeared in England while the latest venture of Samuel Green, the Cambridge, Massachusetts, printer, was a revision of *The Bay Psalm Book*, to rid it of its crudities, gives an indication of the intellectual distance between the two countries). Anne's family, obviously proud of her verse, apparently connived in the printing of it, feeling it deserved a wider audience than it could find among her friends and neighbors. That she was actually unaware of their intention seems clear from the poem "The Author to her Book" (which will be discussed later), expressing embarrassment at its appearance ("snatcht from thence by friends, less wise than true") and her chagrin at its "raggs," or typographical errors.

If the social and psychological forces behind *The Tenth Muse* seem to require somewhat more explanation, it is probably because we have had such a narrow and stereotyped view of Puritanism and of the American Puritans in particular. We have so long colored our views of Puritanism with witch-craft imagery (which, however deep its impact, was not the whole of Puritanism and fortunately came many years later than Anne Bradstreet's less complicated age) that we forget there was a whole generation of colonists who were not frontier-born and educated, but were English citizens, children of the Renaissance, with backgrounds not unlike that of their exact contemporary, John Milton. They grew up in the age of Shakespeare (Anne was born in 1612, the year Shakespeare stopped writing for the theater), the period of the King James version of the Bible. Many of them, like Simon Bradstreet, were college-educated, at England's best universities, in a time of rapidly expanding knowledge. If in that strange period there was a shift in interest, in Douglas Bush's phrase, to "the pious activities of every day," there was not therefore any reason to abandon the extremely high level of learning they had known. Nor was there any reason for persons bred on the King James version of the Bible to forgo their delight, within appropriate bounds, in the many resources of language. Shakespeare might be frowned upon (though there is reason to believe with Josephine Piercy that Anne Bradstreet read him), but every schoolboy in New

England read Cicero, Ovid, Aristotle, the Greek dramatists, Hesiod, and Homer, and kept more salacious material, usually, in his desk. Schools were everywhere, Harvard itself being founded in 1636, a bare six years after the colonists' first Massachusetts winter. If Puritanism seems to us today harsh and rigid, we must remember that in its own time it represented, in Samuel Eliot Morison's phrase, a *via media*, a moderate position between the extremes of Presbyterianism and the separatists.

It was *drama*, therefore, of the Jacobean type that was suspect to the Puritans, and not all the arts. Indeed, if some arts were suppressed, others—like poetry—seemed to flourish. Lady Mary Montagu's later statement that in England "poetry had become as common as taking snuff" was even truer in Puritan New England, where every man seemed, however austere his appearance, to be carrying an unfinished poem in his pocket. Peter Bulkeley, John Cotton, John Eliot—all wrote poetry, including even Anne Bradstreet's father. Thomas Dudley (the severe Thomas Dudley to some, but not to Anne) wrote a poem "On the State of Europe" which was commended by King James, and a long one entitled "On the Four Parts of the World," concerning, apparently, "four Sisters cloth'd in black and white." In Puritan New England every tombstone held verse, every psalm was available in verse form, however "hammered on an anvil" it might be in *The Bay Psalm Book*. The Puritan era, from Michael Wigglesworth's *The Day of Doom* to what Taine called "the Protestant epic of damnation and grace," *Paradise Lost*, was an age of great delight and variety in the creation of verse.

It has been said that Puritan verse was limited to four types: transcriptions of Biblical passages, didactic verse for teaching children, religious lyrics, and polemical verse. However, many amorous poems have been found, elegiac poems, and Virgilian eclogues like Daniel Russell's. Anne's own frank poems expressing physical love for her husband and such nature poems as "Contemplations" go far beyond these four Puritan categories.

There was not, however, much yet of that spirit which was then sweeping English and European verse and causing all the young poets to write verse which we now call metaphysical —such verse as Edward Taylor (in 1671 the new young minister at Westfield, Massachusetts) would write in his notebooks every night. There is little of this complexity in Puritan verse, and little indeed in Anne Bradstreet's own verse—other than in an occasional poem or two such as "As loving Hind" (p. 41), so that it amuses us that she was once dismissed as "one of the fantasticks." While there is much variation in her work, from the rich texture of the "Contemplations" to the stark, quiet tone of her prayers (p. 61), her verse inclines in general to, in Austin Warren's words, the simple, unfigured and unpretentious. For Puritanism preferred, of course, in its verse, as in its prose, the "plain style."

> God's altar needs not our polishing [wrote Richard Mather in the preface to *The Bay Psalm Book*]. We have respected rather a plain translation than to smooth our verses with the sweetness of any paraphrase: and so have attended conscience rather than elegance, fidelity rather than poetry.

In *The Tenth Muse*, written before she was thirty and hardly her best work, Anne Bradstreet aimed slightly higher than this, at creating poetry, though there were some who said she was merely versifying all that she had read. Even such an aim would not be negligible, since the poems indicate some knowledge of, for example, besides the Bible, Burton's *Anatomy of Melancholy*, Florio's Montaigne, Chapman's Homer, Pemble's *Period of the Persian Monarchy*, Dr. Crooke's *Description of the Body of Man*, Archbishop Usher's *Annals of the World*, Ralegh's *History of the World*, Speed's

History of Great Britaine, Camden's *Britannia* and *Annales*, together with such favorite poets as Spenser, Sidney, Drayton, Browne, Wither, and perhaps Quarles.

It was not the first time that the title "Tenth Muse" had been applied to a woman since the Greeks used it of Sappho—it had been given to four Frenchwomen before Anne. Nor was Anne's in fact a unique appearance of a woman poet writing in English. Katherine Phillips, the "Matchless Orinda," was much admired in seventeenth-century London, though her work is little read today. But Anne was the first resident of North America to appear in verse and probably, as Rufus Griswold later held, the best "poet of her sex who wrote in the English language before the end of the seventeenth century."

That she herself realized it was something new and different for a woman to write, she makes clear in her introductory lines ("The Prologue"):

> To sing of Wars, of Captains, and of Kings,
> Of cities founded, Common-wealths begun,
> For my mean pen are too superiour things . . .

To be a poet, furthermore, will bring her and has already brought the contempt of her neighbors:

> I am obnoxious to each carping tongue
> Who says my hand a needle better fits. . . .

In another poem she had been flippant about her sex:

> Yet great *Augustus* was content (we know)
> To be saluted by a silly Crow;
> Then let such Crowes as I, thy praises sing,
> A Crow's a Crow, and *Caesar* is a King.

But here her tone is an earnest (though perhaps tongue-in-cheek) one; she is to be taken for what she is:

>Let Greeks be Greeks, and women what they are . . .
>Preheminence in all and each is yours [man's];
>Yet grant some small acknowledgement of ours.

The Tenth Muse itself consists largely of four long poems (or quaternions), each consisting of four parts. The quaternions are: "The Four Elements," "Of the four Humours," "Of the four Ages of Man," and "The four Seasons of the Year." To these are added a few short poems—"A Dialogue Between Old England and New"; elegies for Sir Philip Sidney, the French Calvinist poet du Bartas, and Queen Elizabeth; transcriptions of two biblical passages; and a long, unfinished poem entitled "The four Monarchyes."

All the four quaternions (reproduced in Part Two of this edition) follow a similar pattern. Four persons, usually sisters, each representing a particular element, season of the year, age or humour of man, meet to debate which is superior. Each is allowed a speech to point out her own good features and the unattractive features of her sisters. There is, as in life, no decision. The sisters call it a draw and gracefully retire undefeated. In all this the tone is argumentative and sharp; the sisters are not very polite with one another. It is interesting to note that Anne Bradstreet herself grew up with four younger sisters in the house.

Her pattern for all this was, of course, her father's poem, "On the Four Parts of the World," where four sisters meet. It would not have been unusual in the seventeenth century, with the current physiological theory of humours and the example of Jonson and others fresh in everyone's mind, to find anyone writing a poem called "Of the four Humours in Mans Constitution." And there was, of course, in an earlier period such debate literature as "The Owl and the Nightingale" and the flytings of John Skelton. But the form of the work was undoubtedly set by the example of her father, that "Magazine of History" whom Anne called her "guide" and "instructor" and from whom, she said, her own love of books had come.

There was another influence, too, whose name has been coupled with Anne Bradstreet's for centuries: that of Guillaume de Salluste du Bartas, the French Calvinist poet whose works *La Semaine* and *La Seconde Semaine* had been translated into English by Josuah Sylvester at the turn of the century (1605) under the title *Du Bartas His Divine Weekes and Workes.* Anne loved the great, sweeping, biblical effects full of what would later be called "poetic diction," and praised extravagantly "Great Bartas sugar'd lines," saying in her elegy upon his death:

> Among the happy wits this age hath shown,
> Great, dear, sweet *Bartas* thou are matchless known.

It is no wonder that Nat Ward in his introductory poem written for *The Tenth Muse* called her a "right *Du Bartas* Girle," a phrase which, unfortunately for a just evaluation of her, stuck. It is true that she admired him, as did for a time Sidney, Spenser, Drayton, and even the young Dryden, none of whom bore a du Bartas label. But the label, for her, was only half-true. If in her early work she was too much under his spell, in her later and better poems she forgot him altogether.

"The Four Elements," the first but by no means most readable of the four quaternions ("Of the four Ages of Man" is easier), is early work and shows Anne imitating Sylvester's pentameter couplets. It sets into motion Empedocles' four elements—fire, earth, water, and air—and solves the problem that had perplexed Greek philosophy since Thales: "which element is superior?" by showing that all are needed. Fire, being most active (it had only recently attempted to destroy "stately London"—a reference to the Great Fire of 1666 apparently added in her revision of the poem), speaks first.

It is not only destructive: it also provides "Your Hooes your Mattocks . . . [to] Subdue the Earth, and fit it for your Grain" or, for the women, "Your Spits, Pots, Jacks . . . [to prepare] Your dayly food." Earth answers her "Cholerick Sister": how would she maintain her fire without earth's fuel? Thus the debate proceeds, each sister pointing out both her constructive and destructive powers, showing that none of the others can get along without her. It is a stiff poem, though not as uninteresting as its critics have maintained. It shows how the Puritans viewed the night sky (with "Planets of both Sexes"), animals (the "Hiæna," "fawning Dog," and "rare found Unicorn"), what they knew perhaps of history ("Spanish and Italian brawles") and geography ("sundry seas, black, white and Adriatique"). It shows a dedicated if not fully developed talent, with a capacity for unusual direct-ness, whether in the unexpectedness of

> Cold sister Earth . . .
> How doth his warmth, refresh thy frozen back

or (in Air's conclusion) the charming naïveté of

> To adde to all I've said was my intent,
> But dare not go beyond my Element.

"Of the four Humours in Mans Constitution" is the longest of the quaternions, and the sharpest in tone. The four ele-ments are replaced by their "daughters," each of whom proves to be one of the four "humours" so important to seventeenth-century physiology. Fire is replaced by Choler, air by Blood, earth by Melancholy, water by Flegme (phlegm). The poem is of most interest to us today in showing that the Puritans were as curious about the new science as anyone else, and also for what it tells of Anne's obsession with anatomy. To read it is to learn what the seventeenth century believed about the body. Of the four humours, Melancholy seems to today's reader to win the argument, if only for its startling castigation of Choler:

> The Kitchin Drudge, the cleanser of the sinks
> That casts out all that man e're eats or drinks:
> If any doubt the truth whence this should come,
> Shew them thy passage to th' Duodenum;
> Thy biting quality still irritates,
> Till filth and thee nature exonerates:
> If there thou'rt stopt, to th' Liver thou turn'st in,
> And thence with jaundies saffrons all the skin.

When Anne writes of "Nor Cough, nor Quinsey, nor the burning Feaver," one should remember that in her own sicknesses (as wept and prayed over in the Religious Meditations of Part One) Anne had a special reason for her interest in disease.

If the writer of "The four Humours" seems perhaps an invalid, that of "Of the four Ages of Man" seems completely a parent. Here, in a much warmer and more personal tone, Childhood, Youth, Middle Age, and Old Age replace the earlier groups. Childhood, while complaining about its "gripes of wind" and the "tortures I in breeding teeth sustain," also has to admit it is far from innocent:

> A serpents sting in pleasing face lay hid.

Youth, often delinquent and "wild as is the snuffing Ass," is described profoundly as being better on the outside ("My goodly cloathing") than on the inside. Middle Age concludes, as did Anne in other poems, that man at his best is vanity. The description of old age is particularly interesting here because the poet has added to it, in her revisions, all the history that the times had recently seen: the "Usurper" Cromwell; a "King by force thrust from his throne." Both the memories of Old Age and the responsibilities of Middle Age suggest the kind of life Thomas Dudley must have led.

"The four Seasons of the Year," last of the completed quaternions, is a familiar subject, which was to become even more familiar in the next century. Spring, Summer, Autumn, Winter take the stage, and while there is some direct observation, as in:

> . . . the early Cherry,
> The hasty Peas, and wholsome cool Strawberry,

there is more imagery that suggests the reading of other poems:

> Now goes the Plow-man to his merry toyle.

The effect is one of tiredness, and indeed the author draws the quaternion to a quick close, saying "My Subjects bare, my Brain is bad."

The longest poem in *The Tenth Muse*, incomplete at more than 4,000 lines, is "The four Monarchyes," which Anne Bradstreet abandoned after her "papers fell a prey to th' raging fire" that destroyed the Bradstreet house in 1666. The poem, which begins with the Assyrian monarchy (rather than with Adam and Eve as many another Puritan poet might have done) and ends, unfinished, with the Romans, was, as John Harvard Ellis pointed out, a metrical restatement of her reading, particularly of Sir Walter Ralegh's *History of the World*. In this edition only one excerpt, in which Belshazzar

> . . . with colour pale and dead
> Then hears his *Mene* and his *Tekel* read,

is given, to suggest that little is lost, other than some unintended humor, in omitting the rest. More than one critic has agreed that the burning of the Bradstreet house and this longest section of *The Tenth Muse* was not entirely a disaster.

Anne Bradstreet's reaction to *The Tenth Muse*, as the book was published in London in 1650, has fortunately been preserved for us in her delightful "The Author to her Book," mentioned before, which introduces (p. 40) the present volume. Her "blushing," she says, "was not small" that her "rambling brat" should appear in print. Like most authors (but with reason in this case) she was horrified at the number of typographical errors, the "raggs" in which it appeared. Nevertheless, with true maternal affection and considerable humor, she sets out to correct them:

> I wash'd thy face, but more defects I saw,
> And rubbing off a spot, still made a flaw.
> I stretcht thy joynts to make thee even feet . . .

But even as revised, apologies may be necessary:

> If for thy Father askt, say thou hadst none:
> And for thy Mother, she alas is poor,
> Which caus'd her thus to send thee out of door.

The period of Anne's revision is about 1666, and it shows her increasing skill in its strengthening of lines and poems. Changes are also made to fit the changing political situation under the rule of Charles II. She can now call Cromwell a "Usurper," reveal her own deep loyalty to England and the crown.

The revised book of Anne Bradstreet's poems, however, was not to appear in her own lifetime. It was published in 1678, six years after her death, as *Several Poems Compiled with great variety of Wit and Learning* . . . "by a Gentlewoman in New-England," and was presented to the public by young John Foster of Boston, whose most important productions up to that time had been John Eliot's *Harmony of the Gospels* and Roger Williams' *George Fox Digg'd out of his Burrowes*. The country was still in its infancy: Cotton Mather was only fifteen, and George Washington's father had not even been born yet.

III

Anne Bradstreet's best work is not in the long poems of *The Tenth Muse*, for all the fame that title was to gather, but in the shorter poems she wrote during her entire lifetime. These poems, left to her children, many of them never intended for publication at all but published only at the insistence of her friends, show quite a different person from the Puritan craftsman spinning her du Bartas allegories. For these shorter works, as assembled in Part One of this edition, show a mature use of poetry to resolve the greatest and most intimate of anxieties by a poet whose deepening seriousness as an artist and person we may ourselves witness.

It is easy, of course, to assign motives to persons long dead, and many have seen in Anne, for example, a political and social rebellion, a general dissatisfaction with the community and public officials of her day. They point out that her father was deputy governor at the time Anne Hutchinson was banished for her antinomian beliefs—indeed, *became* deputy governor when John Wheelwright, Anne Hutchinson's brother-in-law, was being tried for similar beliefs. Mrs. Bradstreet, the argument goes, could not have helped being shaken by the situation, particularly when her own belief might have seemed even more heretical than Mrs. Hutchinson's. She therefore kept silent, but used poetry as her outlet for the resulting tensions, as a way of retaining her sanity in a new world where her "heart rose."

Certainly there is much to be said for the theory. There are veiled hints of the lack of freedom to speak freely, even for the governor's daughter and the wife of the governor-to-be:

> What are my thoughts, this is no time to say.
> Men may more freely speak another day.

Anne Bradstreet would not have been the first woman to think one thing and say another. One does wonder, however, if her feelings for her father and husband—both of whom held positions of great authority—would have remained quite so free and open if she were nursing a long resentment against the New England authorities. We would know better if we had all of her papers instead of only a part.

One concern she did put on paper, however, so that we have poem after poem which treats of it—and this is her quarrel, not with the leaders of the community, but with her God. The Puritan, in his hope, like Calvin, to stress the perfection and holiness of God, had to believe that God had power to cause all events, or, barring that, had foreknowledge of them, so that He knew ahead of time what would happen and allowed it to happen—no matter how dreadful the event— for the good of the individual soul. Indeed, the events of this life were only important as they revealed, bit by bit, God's will and plan. Thus, in writing of the burning of the Bradstreet house, the son Simon wrote:

> . . . the Lord gave, and the Lord hath taken, blessed bee the Name of the Lord.

And Anne herself, in the touching poem "Upon the burning of our house" (p. 54), wrote:

> I blest his Name that gave and took,
> That layd my goods now in the dust:
> Yea so it was, and so 'twas just.
> It was his own: it was not mine.

She had already written, in the manuscript book she kept for her children, with remarkable candor (for a Puritan woman) of her struggles with atheism:

> Many times hath Satan troubled me concerning the verity of the scriptures, many times by Atheisme how I could know whether there was a God; I never saw any miracles to confirm me . . .

"Yet have I many Times sinkings and droopings," she writes elsewhere.

It is especially cruel when illnesses, her own included, must be assigned to the will of God: if He did not cause them to happen, He meant her to learn from them. So from her own bed or children's sickbeds "have I gone to searching, and have said with David, Lord search me and try me, see what wayes of wickednes are in me. . . ." Many of the Religious Meditations beginning on page 61 are of this type. The titles or first lines say it all: "For Deliverance from a feaver," "From another sore Fitt," "For the restoration of my dear Husband from a burning Ague, June, 1661." A lifetime of pain is told in these few poems.

But what of death—not the deaths of her parents, which can be expected, but the deaths of little children? She wrote, as we have mentioned, three such poems, which are to be found beginning on page 57, and, together with a fourth, on her daughter-in-law, are among the most moving poems in our language. "Farewel dear babe, my hearts too much content," she writes to one grandchild, Elizabeth. The second, young Anne, named for her, is "Like as a bubble, or the brittle glass." But with the third, her grandchild Simon, "but a moneth, and one day old," one feels that, for all her saying the "right thing," she can no longer praise such a God and is near to breaking:

> No sooner come, but gone, and fal'n asleep,
> Acquaintance short, yet parting caus'd us weep,
> Three flours, two scarcely blown, the last i'th' bud
> Cropt by th' Almighties hand; yet is he good,
> With dreadful awe before him let's be mute,
> Such was his will, but why, let's not dispute,
> With humble hearts and mouths put in the dust,
> Let's say he's merciful as well as just. . . .

The astonishing thing for the Puritans was that their griefs and doubts *were* overcome in the love-hate relationship that permitted them swiftly to build civilizations on the one hand and cast out heretics and witches on the other. Thus Anne's summary shows daily rather than lifelong rebellions:

> He hath never suffered me long to sitt loose from him. . . .
>
> I have had great experience of God's hearing my Prayers. . . .
>
> I have somtimes tasted of that hidden Manna that the world knowes not. . . .

Her masterwork, the "Contemplations," shows all doubts resolved, and her final poem, the splendid "As weary pilgrim, now at rest," reproduced in her own hand on pages 38 and 39, shows her confident that

> A Corrupt Carcasse downe it lyes
> a glorious body it shall rise . . .

The poems in Part One are arranged by type, so that the reader can see Anne Bradstreet's development in works of considerable variety. The poems are, except as specified, in chronological order within each section.

The five love poems in section I (none intended of course for any eye but her husband's) will surprise those readers whose ideas of Puritanism have stressed only its harsher accents. For here, as in the strong poem "To my Dear and loving Husband," an anthology piece almost Donne-like in the precision and daring of its lines, she writes happily of a love that seems not only spiritual (a theme to be repeated later in "The Flesh and the Spirit") but physical:

> Then while we live, in love lets so persever,
> That when we live no more, we may live ever.

"As loving Hind," her most truly "metaphysical" work, uses the imagery of the deer, the turtledove, and the mullet, but with considerable skill and charm:

> Return my Dear, my joy, my only Love,
> Unto thy Hind, thy Mullet and thy Dove . . .

The poems "Phœbus make haste" and "A Letter to her Husband" explore, in different ways, her loneliness when her husband is away:

> How stayest thou there, whilst I at *Ipswich* lye?

The final poem in this section, "Before the Birth of one of her Children," seems a unique document in our letters, showing her fears of death in childbirth and her concern for her children if her husband should marry again:

> Look to my little babes my dear remains.
> And if thou love thy self, or loved'st me
> These O protect from step Dames injury.

Her husband did remarry, but that was not until some thirty years later and four years after her own death, when he was in his seventy-third year.

The poems in section II, entitled here "Domestic Poems," show her relationship to her home—to her children, parents, and grandchildren. The poems of grief (pp. 57–59) have already been discussed. Here one can find her at the age of nineteen worrying that she may die:

> Twice ten years old, not fully told . . .
> lo here is fatal Death,

or years later recovering from another illness:

> In tossing slumbers on my wakeful bed,
> Bedrencht with tears . . .

Here one can find an elegy to her father—formal but strong in its handling of the conventional manner:

> Within this Tomb a Patriot lyes
> That was both pious, just and wise,
> To truth a shield, to right a Wall,
> To Sectaryes a whip and Maul.

There is one as well for Anne's mother that is nearly perfect in its own quiet way:

A Worthy Matron of unspotted life . . .

Its fourteen lines are all we know of the subject, and to our knowledge all that Anne ever wrote of her.

Of particular interest in this group, however, is the poem already mentioned: "In reference to her Children," beginning "I had eight birds." Here, in a totally delightful manner that seems all her own, she presents, in 94 lines, a successfully sustained metaphor which is never forced, presenting each of her children as a bird who seems intent on leaving the nest:

One to the Academy flew . . .

I have a third of colour white . . .

She worries about their safety and hopes they will remember they had a Dam that loved them well. One can think of few more charming poems of this period; readers new to Anne Bradstreet might well read it first.

Most of the religious poems in section III were found among Anne Bradstreet's papers. They were never intended for publication. They are included in the small manuscript book of her work, where her son Simon carefully transcribed them. Most are written to simple hymn meters, but are not intended as hymns. Rather, they are so personal, almost unbearably so at times, that to read them seems to be eavesdropping on a private conversation between the soul and God. "As weary pilgrim," already mentioned, which closes the group, is of a different kind: an attempt to give a formal and final statement of the soul's yearning for death, written out of great pain and great faith.

The "Contemplations," presented here in section IV, represents the high point of Anne Bradstreet's work, the culmination of her many years of development as a poetic craftsman. This is a long poem of thirty-three connected stanzas (many of which have appeared in anthologies as isolated poems) each (with one exception) of seven lines: six lines of iambic pentameter and a closing alexandrine. The rhyme scheme is an outgrowth of the rhyme royal Chaucer used in *Troilus*, but now rhymed *ababccc* to close with a triplet rather than a couplet. The final stanza, stanza 33, has an additional line and consists of four couplets.

The poem is something that had not yet been heard in New England and was not yet to be heard anywhere for another century to this degree: a nature poem, in which nature is examined and enjoyed for its own sake, and not solely for whatever spiritual messages it contains. Not that the poet forgets in her later years that she is a Puritan; it is simply that here the physical and spiritual are perfectly fused.

The poem describes a walk, either real or imaginary, along the edge of the forest near the Bradstreet home in North Andover, and by the side of the rushing Merrimack. It is autumn and the central figure is "Rapt . . . at this delectable view."

> If so much excellence abide below;
> How excellent is he that dwells on high?

With this question in mind she looks, in turn, at "a stately Oak," "the glistering Sun," "the merry grashopper." Each makes her think of the length of eternity, the numbered years of human life and, for the most part, their waste:

> Living so little while we are alive.

She turns to the nearby river

> Under the cooling shadow of a stately Elm . . .

to fix her eye on the "stealing stream." Here, too, in the examples of "Ye Fish" and "merry Bird" she sees an animal world at peace with itself. Only man, "at the best a creature frail and vain," seems out of harmony; he does not even glory that he will someday be transformed in another life. It is Time at last which conquers all earthly things:

> O Time the fatal wrack of mortal things,
> That draws oblivions curtains over kings . . .

The poem has been much noted because it anticipates the Romantics and contains two lines ("If winter come . . . A Spring returns") that suggest remarkably the more famous line of Shelley. But it should be appreciated for its own sake: the limpid sounds, the quiet effects, its tenderness, lines one can only finally quote in admiration:

More Heaven than Earth was here no winter and no night . . .

Silent alone, where none or saw, or heard . . .

When I behold the heavens as in their prime . . .

or that wonderful cry of humanity driven to its limits:

> But Ah, and Ah, again, my imbecility!

The poems in section V are dialogues that suggest the longer quaternions in Part Two. In "The Flesh and the Spirit," probably a setting of the eighth chapter of *Romans*, Flesh and Spirit, in a near-perfect poem, debate as do the sisters in the quaternions. Spirit of course wins, as one would expect in Puritan New England, but it is interesting to note that Flesh is not simply despised:

> Sister, quoth Flesh, what liv'st thou on
> Nothing but Meditation?

Included here also are poems of similar tone, the well-known "Vanity of all worldly things" and "David's Lamentation for Saul and Jonathan," both from *The Tenth Muse* and excellent examples of their type.

Also from *The Tenth Muse* is the historically interesting

"Dialogue between Old *England* and New; concerning their present Troubles, *Anno*, 1642." Because it was written when one king's life was in danger and revised after another king had been restored to the throne, it claims additional interest by showing how the Colonists felt about the mother country, what they knew of events there, how they thought of themselves. It is apparent from Anne Bradstreet's tone that her relationship toward England was a much more loving one than we might suppose, that she hoped originally Parliament would prevail but only by making peace with Charles I, that she later either changed her views or felt more free to express them in supporting the throne. The poem is serious in mood, but some sardonic humor comes through. The Puritans' adversary Archbishop Laud had been arrested, and she allows herself a pun at his expense:

> And to their *Laud* be't spoke, they held i'th tower
> All *Englands* Metropolitane that hour . . .

The Puritans were fond of formal elegies, and section VI, which closes the first part of the book, consists of three that originally appeared in *The Tenth Muse*. They are in her early manner, full of such instant history as

> *Dido* first Foundress of proud *Carthage* walls,
> (Who living consummates her Funeralls),

but they do show her enthusiasm for three figures—a woman and two poets. Queen Elizabeth she admires because she shows what a woman can do:

> Now say, have women worth? or have they none?
> Or had they some, but with our Queen is't gone?
> Nay Masculines, you have thus taxt us long . . .

Sir Philip Sidney she mourns as did most other poets of the time, because of his brilliance and early death. The poem is conventional in imagery but interesting in showing her identification at a young age with literature hardly representative of the "plain style."

Her elegy to du Bartas goes to the other extreme, of praising an unfortunate influence. It is, however, honest in its praise, and no student of her work or of the period would want to neglect it. In its original appearance it was placed between the other two elegies, but is here placed last, since it provides a transition and introduction to the *Tenth Muse* poems which follow and complete the present edition.

Anne Bradstreet wrote not only poetry but also prose, among it some of the best prose of her generation. Examples are shown in Appendix B (p. 187). It was not unusual for people of that time to keep books in which they wrote down their thoughts, and Anne herself, in a note to her son Simon, said she was leaving these "Meditations" for him and the other children to "look upon when you should see me no more." Few, however, would have presented their children aphorisms so beautifully worded:

> The finest bread hath the least bran; the purest hony, the least wax; and the sincerest christian, the least self love.

The examples of Bacon's essays and Quarles's emblems were probably known to her, but the chief source seems to be the book of Proverbs:

> An akeing head requires a soft pillow; and a drooping heart a strong support.

They are not the essays of a prose stylist but the reflections of a woman of the frontier who has experienced much and thought long about the meaning of life:

> Some Children are hardly weaned, although the teat be rub'd with wormwood or mustard, they wil either wipe it off, or else suck down some sweet and bitter together; so it is with some Christians, let God imbitter all the sweets of this life . . .

And here too she sums up the struggle with God that seems to have been decided, finally, in God's favor:

> Somtimes the sun is only shadowed by a cloud that wee cannot se his luster, although we may walk by his light . . . so God doth somtime vaile his face but for a moment, that we cannot behold the light of his Countenance as at some other time, yet he affords so much light as may direct our way, that we may go forwards to the Citty of habitation.

IV

Estimates of Anne Bradstreet's work have varied according to the generation making them. The long poems—the quaternions—appealed to her contemporaries because they were useful—they combined instruction with beauty. It is doubtful whether many at that time gave much thought to her shorter poems, some of which, indeed, were not made public until John Harvard Ellis's edition in 1867.

Three years after her death Milton's nephew Edward Phillips, in his *Theatrum Poetarium* (1675) showed that her work was not forgotten in England:

> *Anne Bradstreet*, a *New-England* poetess, no less in title . . . the memory of which poems . . . is not yet wholly extinct.

Cotton Mather, writing in his *Magnalia Christi Americana* (1702), spoke of her in glowing terms:

> It must now be said that a Judge of *New England*, namely, *Thomas Dudley*, Esq; had a *Daughter* . . . to be a *Crown* unto him. . . . whose *Poems*, divers times Printed, have afforded a grateful Entertainment unto the Ingenious, and a Monument for her Memory beyond the Statliest *Marbles*.

John Rogers, president of Harvard from 1682 to 1684, wrote a poem about her, and Mrs. Makin, in her British *Essay to Revive the Ancient Education of Gentlewomen*, spoke of "Anne Bradstreet (now in America)" as "an excellent poet."

The number of editions of her work (see Bibliography, p. 215) and the fact that Rufus Griswold, in his *Female Poets of America* (1849), could call her superior to Dame Juliana Berners and the other women poets writing in English up to the beginning of the eighteenth century, would seem to show that she still had a following. One would like to think that the Romantic poets she foreshadowed read her, since (in addition to the Shelley parallel already noted) there are possible echoes in the work of Wordsworth, Coleridge, and Emerson, though influences of this kind are always difficult to establish.

There is no doubt, however, that by the end of the nineteenth century her work had fallen into neglect and disfavor. There were those who followed the Johnsonian line of hating all metaphysical verse—like Moses Coit Tyler in his great survey of Colonial literature, where he indifferently condemns her along with Donne, Herbert, and Crashaw for writing "works of fantastic perversion, and . . . total absence of all beauty." She was, Tyler says, "sadly misguided by the poetic standards of her religious sect and of her literary period." One hardly knows how to begin answering such an attack.

There were those, too, who wrote about her without knowing all her work (such as perhaps one reference book in current use which speaks of her "feeble imitations of Spenser" and lays on her frail shoulders the blame for the entire Brahmin tradition in America!). Finally there were those like her descendant Charles Eliot Norton of Harvard who were embarrassed by her *lack* of learning and the general deplorable work of early-day America. She knew little, he said, besides three books: *The Faerie Queene*, *Arcadia*, and Plutarch. She had little wit, "little playfulness"; one winced at her misspellings. He then proceeded to correct her spelling and punctuation while including, with dubious scholarship of his own, photographs of a house that was not hers and a likeness that was not hers either.

The excellent edition of her work by John Harvard Ellis which appeared in 1867 could not make much headway against this type of prejudice, and it has remained for our own time, with its greater understanding and appreciation of seventeenth-century verse, to give Anne Bradstreet the acclaim she deserves.

In 1930, Conrad Aiken, who also played so important a part in the Emily Dickinson rediscovery, published twelve pages of Anne Bradstreet's poetry, including the complete "Contemplations," in his *Comprehensive Anthology of American Poetry*. Samuel Eliot Morison, in his *Builders of the Bay Colony* (1930), praised her highly, as did Perry Miller in his writings about the Puritans. Her work was effectively presented alongside Milton's and Edward Taylor's in the Viking five-volume *Poets of the English Language*, edited by W. H. Auden and Norman Holmes Pearson.

It was in 1950, on the three-hundredth anniversary of the publication of *The Tenth Muse*, that, through the enthusiasm of Mr. and Mrs. Buchanan Charles and the support of Miss Elizabeth Wade White, Clifton Waller Barrett, Lessing J. Rosenwald, and others, the 98-page manuscript book kept by Mrs. Bradstreet and completed by her son Simon was returned to North Andover, its original home, to be preserved in the collection of the Stevens Memorial Library.

Six years later, in 1956, appeared John Berryman's brilliant *Homage to Mistress Bradstreet*, which Edmund Wilson called the most distinguished long poem by an American since *The Waste Land*—a biographically rich interior monologue that draws on most of Anne Bradstreet's poems and suggests, in its fifty-seven eight-line stanzas, the form of the "Contemplations." In 1965 appeared the excellent study, *Anne Bradstreet*, by Josephine K. Piercy, and in recent years (see Bibliography) there have been perceptive discussions by Elizabeth Wade White, Harold S. Jantz, Ann Stanford, and others. A biography has been announced, and a complete edition of prose and verse, edited by Jeannine Hensley, appeared while this edition was in preparation. The Anne Bradstreet revival is no longer a thing of the future; it is already here.

A final evaluation of her work, of course, remains to be made. It is understandable that many have been drawn to her because she illustrates certain problem areas: the question of early American art, the problem of the woman writer in America. Her two claims to fame—being a woman poet and being America's first poet—have ironically kept many from evaluating her work on its own merits. In England, for example, she is hardly mentioned, though she was as much an English poet as was, say, George Sandys, who also wrote poems in America.

In a similar manner we ourselves may be attracted to her work because it seems to stand for certain virtues—restraint, courage, dignity—in a time of great moral uncertainty and change. Her work needs no such special pleading. We can see many things in it: the hand of a craftsman, the hand of a primitive—someone who successfully makes domestic concerns a subject for poetry—so long as we remember that we are talking about a poet whose works were written primarily to be enjoyed.

The revaluation of Anne Bradstreet will not come until her work is easily accessible for readers of verse and until the best of it has been separated from what will interest primarily the scholar. This edition cannot pretend to be a work of original scholarship, but it does hope to present, in the original spellings and punctuation, poems that have frequently been available only in expensive library editions, and there surrounded by the bulk of her less vital verse. Anne Bradstreet needs to be read at her best. Hopefully, this small volume will help to make this reading possible.

New York, New York   ROBERT HUTCHINSON
1968

33

A NOTE ON THE TEXT

In general, the text is that of the John Harvard Ellis edition of Anne Bradstreet's works, published in Cambridge, Massachusetts, in 1867. There are basically three sources for Anne Bradstreet's work (see Bibliography, p. 215):

The Tenth Muse, London, 1650 (the first edition).

Several Poems, a revision and enlargement of the above book, published posthumously in Boston in 1678 (the second edition). (A so-called third edition which appeared in Boston in 1758 was little more than a reprint of the second.)

The Works of Anne Bradstreet in Prose and Verse, edited by John Harvard Ellis and published in Cambridge for Abram E. Cutter of Charlestown, 1867.

The Ellis edition, based on the 1678 second edition, is followed here.

Some copies of the 1678 edition, including that of the New York Public Library, contain an errata leaf, which originally appeared in complete form only in the Prince copy at the Boston Public Library. Corrections from this errata leaf are included here and are so marked.

The original spelling has been preserved, with a few minor exceptions. I have changed *u*, *v*, and the long *s* in accordance with the customary modern usage. I have also, for the sake of clarity, changed *then* to *than* throughout when such was its meaning. Since seventeenth-century punctuation has its own logic, it was felt better not to change it except in flagrant instances recorded in the Notes. The Notes suggest ways of reading certain lines where punctuation is confusing.

Much of the interest in studying Anne Bradstreet is in noticing how she altered her poems—often because of the changed political circumstances—when preparing them for republication. Significant variations of this type are mentioned in the Notes, though by no means all such changes. A very few readings of the 1650 edition which seemed preferable to the 1678 edition have been retained; all such instances are recorded in the Notes.

All poems are presented in their entirety, with the exception of "The four Monarchyes," a poem of extreme length and somewhat minor poetic interest. Those wishing to read it in its entirety may find it in *The Works of Anne Bradstreet in Prose and Verse*, John Harvard Ellis, ed. (reprinted by Peter Smith, Gloucester, Mass., 1962), where also may be found the whole of the prose "Meditations," here given in part. This edition was nearing completion when the 1967 edition of Anne Bradstreet's poems, edited by Jeannine Hensley and published by Harvard University Press (see Bibliography), was announced. That edition appeared too late to be of any but last-minute assistance; however, I am indebted to it for clarification concerning the 1678 errata leaf.

For permission to reproduce the MS poem I am indebted to The Stevens Memorial Library, North Andover, Massachusetts, owner of the Bradstreet manuscript book, and to its former trustee, Buchanan Charles, who also kindly offered me transcripts of the manuscript book and acquainted me with discrepancies between the handwritten version and Ellis's. I am indebted furthermore to E. F. Bleiler, Clarence Strowbridge and Stanley Appelbaum for suggestions concerning the editing of the poems; to Josephine K. Piercy for her excellent *Anne Bradstreet* (Twayne's United States Author Series), 1965; and to Ann Stanford and Elizabeth Wade White for perceptive studies of Anne Bradstreet and her times. Finally, I owe a special debt of gratitude to Mr. and Mrs. Hayward Cirker, whose sympathetic interest in this project has made the present edition possible.

Part One
SHORTER POEMS

Facsimile of the poem "As weary pilgrim, now at rest" (page 77), as it appears in the Bradstreet manuscript book in the possession of the Stevens Memorial Library, North Andover, Massachusetts. This

This body shall in silence sleep
Mine eyes no more shall weep
No fainting fits shall me assail
nor grinding pains my body frail
W[i]th cares and fears nere combred be
Nor losses know, nor sorrows see
And when this my flesh shall there consume
it is the bed christ did perfume
And when a few yeurs shall be gone
this mortall shall be cloth'd upon
The Corrupted Carcasse downe it lyes
a glorious body it shall rise
In weaknes and dishonour sowne
in power tis raisd by christ alone
Then soule and body shall vnite
and of their maker have the sight
Such lasting ioyes shall there behold
as eare nere heard nor tongue ere told
Lord make me ready for that day
then Come deare bridgrome Come away

Aug: 31 61

is the only poem extant in Anne Bradstreet's own handwriting. The lower left-hand corner of the first page is flawed in the original. Used by permission.

The Author to her Book

Thou ill-form'd offspring of my feeble brain,
Who after birth did'st by my side remain,
Till snatcht from thence by friends, less wise than true
Who thee abroad, expos'd to publick view;
Made thee in raggs, halting to th' press to trudg,
Where errors were not lessened (all may judg)
At thy return my blushing was not small,
My rambling brat (in print) should mother call,
I cast thee by as one unfit for light,
Thy Visage was so irksome in my sight;   10
Yet being mine own, at length affection would
Thy blemishes amend, if so I could:
I wash'd thy face, but more defects I saw,
And rubbing off a spot, still made a flaw.
I stretcht thy joynts to make thee even feet,
Yet still thou run'st more hobling than is meet;
In better dress to trim thee was my mind,
But nought save home-spun Cloth, i'th' house I find.
In this array, 'mongst Vulgars mayst thou roam
In Criticks hands, beware thou dost not come;   20
And take thy way where yet thou art not known,
If for thy Father askt, say, thou hadst none:
And for thy Mother, she alas is poor,
Which caus'd her thus to send thee out of door.

I / LOVE POEMS

To my Dear and loving Husband

If ever two were one, then surely we.
If ever man were lov'd by wife, then thee;
If ever wife was happy in a man,
Compare with me ye women if you can.
I prize thy love more than whole Mines of gold,
Or all the riches that the East doth hold.
My love is such that Rivers cannot quench,
Nor ought but love from thee, give recompence.
Thy love is such I can no way repay,
The heavens reward thee manifold I pray.   10
Then while we live, in love lets so persever,
That when we live no more, we may live ever.

"As loving Hind"

As loving Hind that (Hartless) wants her Deer,
Scuds through the woods and Fern with harkning ear,
Perplext, in every bush and nook doth pry,
Her dearest Deer, might answer ear or eye;
So doth my anxious soul, which now doth miss,
A dearer Dear (far dearer Heart) than this,
Still wait with doubts, and hopes, and failing eye,
His voice to hear, or person to discry.
Or as the pensive Dove doth all alone
(On withered bough) most uncouthly bemoan   10
The absence of her Love, and loving Mate,
Whose loss hath made her so unfortunate:

Ev'n thus doe I, with many a deep sad groan
Bewail my turtle true, who now is gone,
His presence and his safe return, still wooes,
With thousand dolefull sighs and mournfull Cooes.
Or as the loving Mullet, that true Fish,
Her fellow lost, nor joy nor life do wish,
But lanches on that shore, there for to dye,
Where she her captive husband doth espy.   20
Mine being gone, I lead a joyless life,
I have a loving phere, yet seem no wife:
But worst of all, to him can't steer my course,
I here, he there, alas, both kept by force:
Return my Dear, my joy, my only Love,
Unto thy Hinde, thy Mullet and thy Dove,
Who neither joyes in pasture, house nor streams,
The substance gone, O me, these are but dreams.
Together at one Tree, oh let us brouze,
And like two Turtles roost within one house,   30
And like the Mullets in one River glide,
Let's still remain but one, till death divide.

{ *Thy loving Love and Dearest Dear,*
{ *At home, abroad, and every where.*

"*Phœbus make haste*"

Phœbus make haste, the day's too long, be gone,
The silent night's the fittest time for moan;
But stay this once, unto my suit give ear,
And tell my griefs in either Hemisphere:
(And if the whirling of thy wheels don't drown'd
The woful accents of my doleful sound),

If in thy swift Carrier thou canst make stay,
I crave this boon, this Errand by the way,
Commend me to the man more lov'd than life,
Shew him the sorrows of his widdowed wife;   10
My dumpish thoughts, my groans, my brakish tears
My sobs, my longing hopes, my doubting fears,
And if he love, how can he there abide?
My Interest's more than all the world beside.
He that can tell the starrs or Ocean sand,
Or all the grass that in the Meads do stand,
The leaves in th' woods, the hail or drops of rain,
Or in a corn-field number every grain,
Or every mote that in the sun-shine hops,
May count my sighs, and number all my drops: 20
Tell him, the countless steps that thou dost trace,
That once a day, thy Spouse thou mayst imbrace;
And when thou canst not treat by loving mouth,
Thy rayes afar, salute her from the south.
But for one moneth I see no day (poor soul)
Like those far scituate under the pole,
Which day by day long wait for thy arise,
O how they joy when thou dost light the skyes.
O *Phœbus*, hadst thou but thus long from thine
Restrain'd the beams of thy beloved shine,   30
At thy return, if so thou could'st or durst
Behold a Chaos blacker than the first.
Tell him here's worse than a confused matter,
His little world's a fathom under water,
Nought but the fervor of his ardent beams
Hath power to dry the torrent of these streams.
Tell him I would say more, but cannot well,
Oppressed minds, abruptest tales do tell.
Now post with double speed, mark what I say,
By all our loves conjure him not to stay.   40

A Letter to her Husband, absent upon Publick employment

My head, my heart, mine Eyes, my life, nay more,
My joy, my Magazine of earthly store,
If two be one, as surely thou and I,
How stayest thou there, whilst I at *Ipswich* lye?
So many steps, head from the heart to sever
If but a neck, soon should we be together:
I like the earth this season, mourn in black,
My Sun is gone so far in's Zodiack,
Whom whilst I 'joy'd, nor storms, nor frosts I felt,
His warmth such frigid colds did cause to melt.   10
My chilled limbs now nummed lye forlorn;
Return, return sweet *Sol* from *Capricorn*;
In this dead time, alas, what can I more
Than view those fruits which through thy heat I bore?
Which sweet contentment yield me for a space,
True living Pictures of their Fathers face.
O strange effect! now thou art *Southward* gone,
I weary grow, the tedious day so long;
But when thou *Northward* to me shalt return,
I wish my Sun may never set, but burn   20
Within the Cancer of my glowing breast,
The welcome house of him my dearest guest.
Where ever, ever stay, and go not thence,
Till natures sad decree shall call thee hence;
Flesh of thy flesh, bone of thy bone,
I here, thou there, yet both but one.

Before the Birth of one of her Children

All things within this fading world hath end,
Adversity doth still our joyes attend;
No tyes so strong, no friends so dear and sweet,
But with deaths parting blow is sure to meet.
The sentence past is most irrevocable,
A common thing, yet oh inevitable;
How soon, my Dear, death may my steps attend,
How soon't may be thy Lot to lose thy friend,
We both are ignorant, yet love bids me
These farewell lines to recommend to thee,   10
That when that knot's unty'd that made us one,
I may seem thine, who in effect am none.
And if I see not half my dayes that's due,
What nature would, God grant to yours and you;
The many faults that well you know I have,
Let be interr'd in my oblivious grave;
If any worth or virtue were in me,
Let that live freshly in thy memory
And when thou feel'st no grief, as I no harms,
Yet love thy dead, who long lay in thine arms: 20
And when thy loss shall be repaid with gains
Look to my little babes my dear remains.
And if thou love thy self, or loved'st me
These O protect from step Dames injury.
And if chance to thine eyes shall bring this verse,
With some sad sighs honour my absent Herse;
And kiss this paper for thy loves dear sake,
Who with salt tears this last Farewel did take.

In reference to her Children, 23. June, 1656

I had eight birds hatcht in one nest,
Four Cocks there were, and Hens the rest,
I nurst them up with pain and care,
Nor cost, nor labour did I spare,
Till at the last they felt their wing,
Mounted the Trees, and learn'd to sing;
Chief of the Brood then took his flight,
To Regions far, and left me quite:
My mournful chirps I after send,
Till he return, or I do end,   10
Leave not thy nest, thy Dam and Sire,
Fly back and sing amidst this Quire.
My second bird did take her flight,
And with her mate flew out of sight;
Southward they both their course did bend,
And Seasons twain they there did spend:
Till after blown by *Southern* gales,
They *Norward* steer'd with filled sayles.
A prettier bird was no where seen,
Along the Beach among the treen.   20
I have a third of colour white,
On whom I plac'd no small delight;
Coupled with mate loving and true,
Hath also bid her Dam adieu:
And where *Aurora* first appears,
She now hath percht, to spend her years;
One to the Academy flew
To chat among that learned crew:
Ambition moves still in his breast

That he might chant above the rest,   30
Striving for more than to do well,
That nightingales he might excell.
My fifth, whose down is yet scarce gone
Is 'mongst the shrubs and bushes flown,
And as his wings increase in strength,
On higher boughs he'l pearch at length.
My other three, still with me nest,
Untill they'r grown, then as the rest,
Or here or there, they'l take their flight,
As is ordain'd, so shall they light.   40
If birds could weep, then would my tears
Let others know what are my fears
Lest this my brood some harm should catch,
And be surpriz'd for want of watch,
Whilst pecking corn, and void of care
They fall un'wares in Fowlers snare:
Or whilst on trees they sit and sing,
Some untoward boy at them do fling:
Or whilst allur'd with bell and glass,
The net be spread, and caught, alas.   50
Or least by Lime-twigs they be foyl'd,
Or by some greedy hawks be spoyl'd.
O would my young, ye saw my breast,
And knew what thoughts there sadly rest,
Great was my pain when I you bred,
Great was my care, when I you fed,
Long did I keep you soft and warm,
And with my wings kept off all harm,
My cares are more, and fears than ever,
My throbs such now, as 'fore were never: 60
Alas my birds, you wisdome want,
Of perils you are ignorant,
Oft times in grass, on trees, in flight,

Sore accidents on you may light.
O to your safety have an eye,
So happy may you live and die:
Mean while my dayes in tunes Ile spend,
Till my weak layes with me shall end.
In shady woods I'le sit and sing,
And things that past, to mind I'le bring.   70
Once young and pleasant, as are you,
But former toyes (no joyes) adieu.
My age I will not once lament,
But sing, my time so near is spent.
And from the top bough take my flight,
Into a country beyond sight,
Where old ones, instantly grow young,
And there with Seraphims set song:
No seasons cold, nor storms they see;
But spring lasts to eternity,   80
When each of you shall in your nest
Among your young ones take your rest,
In chirping language, oft them tell,
You had a Dam that lov'd you well,
That did what could be done for young,
And nurst you up till you were strong,
And 'fore she once would let you fly,
She shew'd you joy and misery;
Taught what was good, and what was ill,
What would save life, and what would kill?   90
Thus gone, amongst you I may live,
And dead, yet speak, and counsel give:
Farewel my birds, farewel adieu,
I happy am, if well with you.

Twice ten years old, not fully told
   Since nature gave me breath,
My race is run, my thread is spun,
   lo here is fatal Death.
All men must dye, and so must I
   this cannot be revok'd
For Adams sake, this word God spake
   when he so high provok'd.
Yet live I shall, this life's but small,
   in place of highest bliss,   10
Where I shall have all I can crave,
   no life is like to this.
For what's this life, but care and strife?
   since first we came from womb,
Our strength doth waste, our time doth hast,
   and then we go to th' Tomb.
O Bubble blast, how long can'st last?
   that alwayes art a breaking,
No sooner blown, but dead and gone,
   ev'n as a word that's speaking.   20
O whil'st I live, this grace me give,
   I doing good may be,
Then deaths arrest I shall count best,
   because it's thy decree;
Bestow much cost there's nothing lost,
   to make Salvation sure,
O great's the gain, though got with pain,
   comes by profession pure.
The race is run, the field is won,
   the victory's mine I see,   30
For ever know, thou envious foe,
   the foyle belongs to thee.

To her Father with some verses

Most truly honoured, and as truly dear,
If worth in me, or ought I do appear,
Who can of right better demand the same?
Than may your worthy self from whom it came.
The principle might yield a greater sum,
Yet handled ill, amounts but to this crum;
My stock's so small, I know not how to pay,
My Bond remains in force unto this day;
Yet for part payment take this simple mite,
Where nothing's to be had Kings loose their right.   10
Such is my debt, I may not say forgive,
But as I can, I'le pay it while I live:
Such is my bond, none can discharge but I,
Yet paying is not payd until I dye.

To the Memory of my dear and ever honoured Father Thomas Dudley Esq; Who deceased, July 31. 1653. and of his Age, 77

By duty bound, and not by custome led,
To celebrate the praises of the dead,
My mournfull mind, sore prest, in trembling verse
Presents my Lamentations at his Herse,
Who was my Father, Guide, Instructer too,
To whom I ought whatever I could doe:
Nor is't Relation near my hand shall tye;
For who more cause to boast his worth than I?
Who heard or saw, observ'd or knew him better?
Or who alive than I, a greater debtor?   10
Let malice bite, and envy knaw its fill,
He was my Father, and Ile praise him still.

Nor was his name, or life lead so obscure
That pitty might some Trumpeters procure,
Who after death might make him falsly seem
Such as in life, no man could justly deem.
Well known and lov'd, where ere he liv'd, by most
Both in his native, and in foreign coast,
These to the world his merits could make known,
So needs no Testimonial from his own;   20
But now or never I must pay my Sum;
While others tell his worth, I'le not be dumb:
One of thy Founders, him *New-England* know,
Who staid thy feeble sides when thou wast low,
Who spent his state, his strength, and years with care
That After-comers in them might have share.
True Patriot of this little Commonweal,
Who is't can tax thee ought, but for thy zeal?
Truths friend thou wert, to errors still a foe,
Which caus'd Apostates to maligne so.   30
Thy love to true Religion e're shall shine,
My Fathers God, be God of me and mine.
Upon the earth he did not build his nest,
But as a Pilgrim, what he had, possest.
High thoughts he gave no harbour in his heart,
Nor honours pufft him up, when he had part:
Those titles loath'd, which some too much do love
For truly his ambition lay above.
His humble mind so lov'd humility,
He left it to his race for Legacy: 40
And oft and oft, with speeches mild and wise,
Gave his in charge, that Jewel rich to prize.
No ostentation seen in all his wayes,
As in the mean ones, of our foolish dayes,
Which all they have, and more still set to view,
Their greatness may be judg'd by what they shew.

His thoughts were more sublime, his actions wise,
Such vanityes he justly did despise.
Nor wonder 'twas, low things ne'r much did move
For he a Mansion had, prepar'd above,   50
For which he sigh'd and pray'd and long'd full sore
He might be cloath'd upon, for evermore.
Oft spake of death, and with a smiling chear,
He did exult his end was drawing near,
Now fully ripe, as shock of wheat that's grown,
Death as a Sickle hath him timely mown,
And in celestial Barn hath hous'd him high,
Where storms, nor showrs, nor ought can damnifie.
His Generation serv'd, his labours cease;
And to his Fathers gathered is in peace.   60
Ah happy Soul, 'mongst Saints and Angels blest,
Who after all his toyle, is now at rest:
His hoary head in righteousness was found:
As joy in heaven on earth let praise resound.
Forgotten never be his memory,
His blessing rest on his posterity:
His pious Footsteps followed by his race,
At last will bring us to that happy place
Where we with joy each others face shall see,
And parted more by death shall never be.   70

His Epitaph

Within this Tomb a Patriot lyes
That was both pious, just and wise,
To Truth a shield, to right a Wall,
To Sectaryes a whip and Maul,
A Magazine of History,
A Prizer of good Company

In manners pleasant and severe
The Good him lov'd, the bad did fear,
And when his time with years was spent
If some rejoyc'd, more did lament.   80

An Epitaph On my dear and ever honoured Mother Mrs.
Dorothy Dudley, who deceased Decemb. 27. 1643. and
of her age, 61

Here lyes,
A Worthy Matron of unspotted life,
A loving Mother and obedient wife,
A friendly Neighbor, pitiful to poor,
Whom oft she fed, and clothed with her store;
To Servants wisely aweful, but yet kind,
And as they did, so they reward did find:
A true Instructer of her Family,
The which she ordered with dexterity.
The publick meetings ever did frequent,
And in her Closet constant hours she spent;   10
Religious in all her words and wayes,
Preparing still for death, till end of dayes:
Of all her Children, Children, liv'd to see,
Then dying, left a blessed memory.

Upon the burning of our house, July 10th, 1666

In silent night when rest I took,
For sorrow neer I did not look,
I waken'd was with thundring nois
And Piteous shreiks of dreadfull voice.
That fearfull sound of fire and fire,
Let no man know is my Desire.

I, starting up, the light did spye,
And to my God my heart did cry
To strengthen me in my Distresse
And not to leave me succourlesse.   10
Then coming out beheld a space,
The flame consume my dwelling place.

And, when I could no longer look,
I blest his Name that gave and took,
That layd my goods now in the dust:
Yea so it was, and so 'twas just.
It was his own: it was not mine;
Far be it that I should repine.

He might of All justly bereft,
But yet sufficient for us left.   20
When by the Ruines oft I past,
My sorrowing eyes aside did cast,
And here and there the places spye
Where oft I sate, and long did lye.

Here stood that Trunk, and there that chest;
There lay that store I counted best:
My pleasant things in ashes lye,
And them behold no more shall I.
Under thy roof no guest shall sitt,
Nor at thy Table eat a bitt.   30

No pleasant tale shall 'ere be told,
Nor things recounted done of old.
No Candle 'ere shall shine in Thee,
Nor bridegroom's voice ere heard shall bee.
In silence ever shalt thou lye;
Adeiu, Adeiu; All's vanity.

Then streight I gin my heart to chide,
And did thy wealth on earth abide?
Didst fix thy hope on mouldring dust,
The arm of flesh didst make thy trust?   40
Raise up thy thoughts above the skye
That dunghill mists away may flie.

Thou hast an house on high erect
Fram'd by that mighty Architect,
With glory richly furnished,
Stands permanent tho' this bee fled.
It's purchaséd, and paid for too
By him who hath enough to doe.

A Prise so vast as is unknown,
Yet, by his Gift, is made thine own.   50
Ther's wealth enough, I need no more;
Farewell my Pelf, farewell my Store.
The world no longer let me Love,
My hope and Treasure lyes Above.

Upon some distemper of body

In anguish of my heart repleat with woes,
And wasting pains, which best my body knows,
In tossing slumbers on my wakeful bed,
Bedrencht with tears that flow'd from mournful head,
Till nature had exhausted all her store,
Then eyes lay dry, disabled to weep more;
And looking up unto his Throne on high,
Who sendeth help to those in misery;
He chac'd away those clouds, and let me see
My Anchor cast i'th' vale with safety.   10
He eas'd my Soul of woe, my flesh of pain,
And brought me to the shore from troubled Main.

In memory of my dear grand-child Elizabeth Bradstreet,
who deceased August, 1665. being a year and a half old

Farewel dear babe, my hearts too much content,
Farewel sweet babe, the pleasure of mine eye,
Farewel fair flower that for a space was lent,
Then ta'en away unto Eternity.
Blest babe why should I once bewail thy fate,
Or sigh thy dayes so soon were terminate;
Sith thou art setled in an Everlasting state.

2

By nature Trees do rot when they are grown.
And Plumbs and Apples throughly ripe do fall,
And Corn and grass are in their season mown,   10
And time brings down what is both strong and tall.
But plants new set to be eradicate,
And buds new blown, to have so short a date,
Is by his hand alone that guides nature and fate.

In memory of my dear grand-child Anne Bradstreet.
Who deceased June 20. 1669. being three years and seven
Moneths old

With troubled heart and trembling hand I write,
The Heavens have chang'd to sorrow my delight.
How oft with disappointment have I met,
When I on fading things my hopes have set?
Experience might 'fore this have made me wise,
To value things according to their price:
Was ever stable joy yet found below,
Or perfect bliss without mixture of woe?

I knew she was but as a withering flour,
That's here to day, perhaps gone in an hour;   10
Like as a bubble, or the brittle glass,
Or like a shadow turning as it was.
More fool then I to look on that was lent,
As if mine own, when thus impermanent.
Farewel dear child, thou ne're shall come to me,
But yet a while, and I shall go to thee;
Mean time my throbbing heart's chear'd up with this
Thou with thy Saviour art in endless bliss.

*On my dear Grand-child Simon Bradstreet, Who dyed
on 16. Novemb. 1669. being but a moneth, and one day
old*

No sooner come, but gone, and fal'n asleep,
Acquaintance short, yet parting caus'd us weep,
Three flours, two scarcely blown, the last i'th' bud,
Cropt by th' Almighties hand; yet is he good,
With dreadful awe before him let's be mute,
Such was his will, but why, let's not dispute,
With humble hearts and mouths put in the dust,
Let's say he's merciful as well as just.
He will return, and make up all our losses,
And smile again, after our bitter crosses.   10
Go pretty babe, go rest with Sisters twain
Among the blest in endless joyes remain.

*To the memory of my dear Daughter in Law, Mrs.
Mercy Bradstreet, who deceased Sept. 6. 1669. in the
28. year of her Age*

And live I still to see Relations gone,
And yet survive to sound this wailing tone;

Ah, woe is me, to write thy Funeral Song,
Who might in reason yet have lived long,
I saw the branches lopt the Tree now fall,
I stood so nigh, it crusht me down withal;
My bruised heart lies sobbing at the Root,
That thou dear Son hath lost both Tree and fruit:
Thou then on Seas sailing to forreign Coast;
Was ignorant what riches thou hadst lost.   10
But ah too soon those heavy tydings fly,
To strike thee with amazing misery;
Oh how I simpathize with thy sad heart,
And in thy griefs still bear a second part:
I lost a daughter dear, but thou a wife,
Who lov'd thee more (it seem'd) than her own life.
Thou being gone, she longer could not be,
Because her Soul she'd sent along with thee.
One week she only past in pain and woe,
And then her sorrows all at once did go;   20
A Babe she left before, she soar'd above,
The fifth and last pledg of her dying love,
E're nature would, it hither did arrive,
No wonder it no longer did survive.
So with her Children four, she's now a rest,
All freed from grief (I trust) among the blest;
She one hath left, a joy to thee and me,
The Heavens vouchsafe she may so ever be.
Chear up, (dear Son) thy fainting bleeding heart,
In him alone, that caused all this smart;   30
What though thy strokes full sad and grievous be,
He knows it is the best for thee and me.

III / RELIGIOUS MEDITATIONS

To my Dear Children

This book by Any yet unread,
I leave for you when I am dead,
That, being gone, here you may find
What was your liveing mother's mind.
Make use of what I leave in Love
And God shall blesse you from above.

"By night when others soundly slept"

I

By night when others soundly slept,
And had at once both ease and Rest,
My waking eyes were open kept,
And so to lye I found it best.

II

I sought him whom my Soul did Love,
With tears I sought him earnestly;
He bow'd his ear down from Above,
In vain I did not seek or cry.

III

My hungry Soul he fill'd with Good,
He in his Bottle putt my teares,   10
My smarting wounds washt in his blood,
And banisht thence my Doubts and feares.

What to my Saviour shall I give,
Who freely hath done this for me?
I'le serve him here whilst I shall live,
And Love him to Eternity.

For Deliverance from a feaver

When Sorrowes had begyrt me round,
    And Paines within and out,
When in my flesh no part was found,
    Then didst thou rid me out.

My burning flesh in sweat did boyle,
    My aking head did break;
From side to side for ease I toyle,
    So faint I could not speak.

Beclouded was my Soul with fear
    Of thy Displeasure sore,   10
Nor could I read my Evidence
    Which oft I read before.

Hide not thy face from me, I cry'd,
    From Burnings keep my soul;
Thou know'st my heart, and hast me try'd;
    I on thy Mercyes Rowl.

O, heal my Soul, thou know'st I said,
    Tho' flesh consume to nought;
What tho' in dust it shall bee lay'd,
    To Glory shall bee brought.   20

Thou heardst, thy rod thou didst remove,
  And spar'd my Body frail,
Thou shew'st to me thy tender Love,
  My heart no more might quail.

O, Praises to my mighty God,
  Praise to my Lord, I say,
Who hath redeem'd my Soul from pitt:
  Praises to him for Aye!

From another sore Fitt

In my distresse I sought the Lord,
When nought on Earth could comfort give;
And when my Soul these things abhor'd,
Then, Lord, thou said'st unto me, Live.

Thou knowest the sorrowes that I felt,
My plaints and Groanes were heard of Thee,
And how in sweat I seem'd to melt;
Thou help'st and thou regardest me.

My wasted flesh thou didst restore,
My feeble loines didst gird with strenght;   10
Yea, when I was most low and poor,
I said I shall praise thee at lenght.

What shall I render to my God
For all his Bounty shew'd to me,
Even for his mercyes in his rod,
Where pitty most of all I see?

My heart I wholly give to Thee:
O make it fruitfull, faithfull Lord!
My life shall dedicated bee
To praise in thought, in Deed, in Word.   20

Thou know'st no life I did require
Longer than still thy Name to praise,
Nor ought on Earth worthy Desire,
In drawing out these wretched Dayes.

Thy Name and praise to celebrate,
O Lord! for aye is my request.
O, graunt I doe it in this state,
And then with thee which is the Best.

Deliverance from a fitt of Fainting

Worthy art Thou, O Lord of praise!
    But ah! it's not in me;
My sinking heart I pray thee raise,
    So shall I give it Thee.

My life as Spider's webb's cutt off,
    Thus fainting have I said,
And liveing man no more shall see,
    But bee in silence layd.

My feblee Spirit thou didst revive,
    My Doubting thou didst chide,   10
And tho' as dead mad'st me alive,
    I here a while might 'bide.

Why should I live but to thy Praise?
    My life is hid with Thee;
O Lord, no longer bee my Dayes,
    Than I may fruitfull bee.

What God is like to him I serve,
   What Saviour like to mine?
O, never let me from thee swerve,
   For truly I am thine.

My thankfull mouth shall speak thy praise,
   My Tongue shall talk of Thee:
On High my heart, O, doe thou raise,
   For what thou'st done for me.

Goe, Worldlings, to your Vanities,
   And heathen to your Gods;   10
Let them help in Adversities,
   And sanctefye their rods.

My God he is not like to yours,
   Your selves shall Judges bee;
I find his Love, I know his Pow'r,
   A Succourer of mee.

He is not man that he should lye,
   Nor son of man to unsay;
His word he plighted hath on high,
   And I shall live for aye.   20

And for his sake that faithfull is,
   That dy'd but now doth live,
The first and last, that lives for aye,
   Me lasting life shall give.

"My soul, rejoice thou in thy God"

My soul, rejoice thou in thy God,
    Boast of him all the Day,
Walk in his Law, and kisse his Rod,
    Cleave close to him alway.

What tho' thy outward Man decay,
    Thy inward shall waxe strong;
Thy body vile it shall bee chang'd,
    And glorious made ere-long.

With Angels-wings thy Soul shall mount
    To Blisse unseen by Eye,   10
And drink at unexhausted fount
    Of Joy unto Eternity.

Thy teares shall All bee dryed up,
    Thy Sorrowes all shall flye;
Thy Sinns shall ne'er bee summon'd up,
    Nor come in memory.

Then shall I know what thou hast done
    For me, unworthy me,
And praise thee shall ev'n as I ought,
    For wonders that I see.   20

Base World, I trample on thy face,
    Thy Glory I despise,
No gain I find in ought below,
    For God hath made me wise.

Come, Jesus, quickly, Blessed Lord,
    Thy face when shall I see?
O let me count each hour a Day
    'Till I dissolved bee.

"As spring the winter doth succeed"

As spring the winter doth succeed,
And leaves the naked Trees doe dresse,
The earth all black is cloth'd in green;
At sun-shine each their joy expresse.

My Suns returned with healing wings,
My Soul and Body doth rejoice;
My heart exults, and praises sings
To him that heard my wailing Voice.

My winters past, my stormes are gone,
And former clowdes seem now all fled;   10
But, if they must eclipse again,
I'le run where I was succoured.

I have a shelter from the storm,
A shadow from the fainting heat;
I have accesse unto his Throne,
Who is a God so wondrous great.

O hast thou made my Pilgrimage
Thus pleasant, fair, and good;
Bless'd me in Youth and elder Age,
My Baca made a springing flood?   20

I studious am what I shall doe,
To show my Duty with delight;
All I can give is but thine own,
And at the most a simple mite.

Upon my Son Samuel his goeing for England, Novem. 6, 1657

Thou mighty God of Sea and Land,
I here resigne into thy hand
The Son of Prayers, of vowes, of teares,
The child I stay'd for many yeares.
Thou heard'st me then, and gav'st him me;
Hear me again, I give him Thee.
He's mine, but more, O Lord, thine own,
For sure thy Grace on him is shown.
No freind I have like Thee to trust,
For mortall helpes are brittle Dust.   10
Preserve, O Lord, from stormes and wrack,
Protect him there, and bring him back;
And if thou shalt spare me a space,
That I again may see his face,
Then shall I celebrate thy Praise,
And Blesse thee for't even all my Dayes.
If otherwise I goe to Rest,
Thy Will bee done, for that is best;
Persuade my heart I shall him see
For ever happefy'd with Thee.   20

"My thankfull heart with glorying Tongue"

My thankfull heart with glorying Tongue
    Shall celebrate thy Name,
Who hath restor'd, redeem'd, recur'd
    From sicknes, death, and Pain.

I cry'd thou seem'st to make some stay,
    I sought more earnestly;
And in due time thou succour'st me,
    And sent'st me help from High.

Lord, whilst my fleeting time shall last,
  Thy Goodnes let me Tell.   10
And new Experience I have gain'd,
  My future Doubts repell.

An humble, faitefull life, O Lord,
  For ever let me walk;
Let my obedience testefye,
  My Praise lyes not in Talk.

Accept, O Lord, my simple mite,
  For more I cannot give;
What thou bestow'st I shall restore,
  For of thine Almes I live.   20

*For the restoration of my dear Husband from a burning
Ague, June, 1661*

When feares and sorrowes me besett,
  Then did'st thou rid me out;
When heart did faint and spirits quail,
  Thou comforts me about.

Thou rais'st him up I feard to loose,
  Regav'st me him again:
Distempers thou didst chase away;
  With strenght didst him sustain.

My thankfull heart, with Pen record
  The Goodnes of thy God;   10
Let thy obedience testefye
  He taught thee by his rod.

And with his staffe did thee support,
   That thou by both may'st learn;
And 'twixt the good and evill way,
   At last, thou mig'st discern.

Praises to him who hath not left
   My Soul as destitute;
Nor turnd his ear away from me,
   But graunted hath my Suit.   20

*Upon my Daughter Hannah Wiggin her recovery from
a dangerous feaver*

Bles't bee thy Name, who did'st restore
   To health my Daughter dear
When death did seem ev'n to approach,
   And life was ended near.

Graunt shee remember what thou'st done,
   And celebrate thy Praise;
And let her Conversation say,
   Shee loves thee all thy Dayes.

On my Sons Return out of England, July 17, 1661

All Praise to him who hath now turn'd
My feares to Joyes, my sighes to song,
My Teares to smiles, my sad to glad:
He's come for whom I waited long.

Thou di'st preserve him as he went;
In raging stormes did'st safely keep:
Did'st that ship bring to quiet Port.
The other sank low in the Deep.

From Dangers great thou did'st him free
Of Pyrates who were neer at hand;   10
And order'st so the adverse wind,
That he before them gott to Land.

In country strange thou did'st provide,
And freinds rais'd him in every Place;
And courtesies of sundry sorts
From such as 'fore nere saw his face.

In sicknes when he lay full sore,
His help and his Physitian wer't;
When royall ones that Time did dye,
Thou heal'dst his flesh, and cheer'd his heart.   20

From troubles and Incūbers Thou,
(Without all fraud), did'st sett him free,
That, without scandall, he might come
To th' Land of his Nativity.

On Eagles wings him hether brought
Thro' Want and Dangers manifold;
And thus hath graunted my Request,
That I thy Mercyes might behold.

O help me pay my Vowes, O Lord!
That ever I may thankfull bee,   30
And may putt him in mind of what
Tho'st done for him, and so for me.

In both our hearts erect a frame
Of Duty and of Thankfullnes,
That all thy favours great receiv'd,
Oure upright walking may expresse.

Upon my dear and loving husband his goeing into England, Jan. 16, 1661

O Thou most high who rulest All,
    And hear'st the Prayers of Thine;
O hearken, Lord, unto my suit,
    And my Petition signe.

Into thy everlasting Armes
    Of mercy I commend
Thy servant, Lord. Keep and preserve
    My husband, my dear freind.

At thy command, O Lord, he went,
    Nor nought could keep him back;   10
Then let thy promis joy his heart:
    O help, and bee not slack.

Upon my heart in Thee, O God,
    Thou art my strenght and stay;
Thou see'st how weak and frail I am,
    Hide not thy face Away.

I, in obedience to thy Will,
    Thou knowest, did submitt;
It was my Duty so to doe,
    O Lord, accept of it.   20

Unthankfullnes for mercyes Past,
    Impute thou not to me;
O Lord, thou know'st my weak desire
    Was to sing Praise to Thee.

Lord, bee thou Pilott to the ship,
    And send them prosperous gailes;
In stormes and sicknes, Lord, preserve.
    Thy Goodnes never failes.

Unto thy work he hath in hand,
    Lord, graunt Thou good Successe   30
And favour in their eyes, to whom
    He shall make his Addresse.

Remember, Lord, thy folk whom thou
    To wildernesse hast brought;
Let not thine own Inheritance
    Bee sold away for Nought.

But Tokens of thy favour Give—
    With Joy send back my Dear,
That I, and all thy servants, may
    Rejoice with heavenly chear.   40

Lord, let my eyes see once Again
    Him whom thou gavest me,
That wee together may sing Praise
    For ever unto Thee.

And the Remainder of oure Dayes
    Shall consecrated bee,
With an engaged heart to sing
    All Praises unto Thee.

In my Solitary houres in my dear husband his Absence

O Lord, thou hear'st my dayly moan,
  And see'st my dropping teares:
My Troubles All are Thee before,
  My Longings and my feares.

Thou hetherto hast been my God;
  Thy help my soul hath found:
Tho' losse and sicknes me assail'd,
  Thro' thee I've kept my Ground.

And thy Abode tho'st made with me;
  With Thee my Soul can talk   10
In secrett places, Thee I find,
  Where I doe kneel or walk.

Tho' husband dear bee from me gone,
  Whom I doe love so well;
I have a more beloved one
  Whose comforts far excell.

O stay my heart on thee, my God,
  Uphold my fainting Soul!
And, when I know not what to doe,
  I'll on thy mercyes roll.   20

My weaknes, thou do'st know full well,
  Of Body and of mind.
I, in this world, no comfort have,
  But what from Thee I find.

Tho' children thou hast given me,
  And freinds I have also:
Yet, if I see Thee not thro' them,
  They are no Joy, but woe.

O shine upon me, blessed Lord,
    Ev'n for my Saviour's sake;   30
In Thee Alone is more than All,
    And there content I'll take.

O hear me, Lord, in this Request,
    As thou before ha'st done:
Bring back my husband, I beseech,
    As thou didst once my Sonne.

So shall I celebrate thy Praise,
    Ev'n while my Dayes shall last;
And talk to my Beloved one
    Of all thy Goodnes past.   40

So both of us thy Kindnes, Lord,
    With Praises shall recount,
And serve Thee better than before,
    Whose Blessings thus surmount.

But give me, Lord, a better heart,
    Then better shall I bee,
To pay the vowes which I doe owe
    For ever unto Thee.

Unlesse thou help, what can I doe
    But still my frailty show?   50
If thou assist me, Lord, I shall
    Return Thee what I owe.

In thankfull acknowledgment for the letters I received from my husband out of England

O Thou that hear'st the Prayers of Thine,
And 'mongst them hast regarded Mine,
Hast heard my cry's, and seen my Teares;
Hast known my doubts and All my Feares.

Thou hast releiv'd my fainting heart,
Nor payd me after my desert;
Thou hast to shore him safely brought
For whom I thee so oft besought.

Thou wast the Pilott to the ship,
And rais'd him up when he was sick;   10
And hope thou'st given of good successe,
In this his Buisnes and Addresse;

And that thou wilt return him back,
Whose presence I so much doe lack.
For All these mercyes I thee Praise,
And so desire ev'n all my Dayes.

In thankfull Remembrance for my dear husbands safe Arrivall Sept. 3, 1662

What shall I render to thy Name,
  Or how thy Praises speak;
My thankes how shall I testefye?
  O Lord, thou know'st I'm weak.

I ow so much, so little can
  Return unto thy Name,
Confusion seases on my Soul,
  And I am fill'd with shame.

O thou that hearest Prayers, Lord,
   To Thee shall come all Flesh;   10
Thou hast me heard and answered,
   My 'Plaints have had accesse.

What did I ask for but thou gav'st?
   What could I more desire?
But Thankfullnes, even all my dayes,
   I humbly this Require.

Thy mercyes, Lord, have been so great,
   In number numberles,
Impossible for to recount
   Or any way expresse.   20

O help thy Saints that sought thy Face,
   T' Return unto thee Praise,
And walk before thee as they ought,
   In strict and upright wayes.

"*As weary pilgrim, now at rest*"

As weary pilgrim, now at rest,
   Hugs with delight his silent nest
His wasted limbes, now lye full soft
   That myrie steps, have troden oft
Blesses himself, to think upon
   his dangers past, and travailes done
The burning sun no more shall heat
   Nor stormy raines, on him shall beat.
The bryars and thornes no more shall scratch
   nor hungry wolves at him shall catch   10

He erring pathes no more shall tread
   nor wild fruits eate, in stead of bread,
for waters cold he doth not long
   for thirst no more shall parch his tongue
No rugged stones his feet shall gaule
   nor stumps nor rocks cause him to fall
All cares and feares, he bids farwell
   and meanes in safity now to dwell.
A pilgrim I, on earth, perplext
   with sinns with cares and sorrows vext   20
By age and paines brought to decay
   and my Clay house mouldring away
Oh how I long to be at rest
   and soare on high among the blest.
This body shall in silence sleep
   Mine eyes no more shall ever weep
No fainting fits shall me assaile
   nor grinding paines my body fraile
With cares and fears ne'r cumbred be
   Nor losses know, nor sorrowes see   30
What tho my flesh shall there consume
   it is the bed Christ did perfume
And when a few yeares shall be gone
   this mortall shall be cloth'd upon
A Corrupt Carcasse downe it lyes
   a glorious body it shall rise
In weaknes and dishonour sowne
   in power 'tis rais'd by Christ alone
Then soule and body shall unite
   and of their maker have the sight   40
Such lasting joyes shall there behold
   as eare ne'r heard nor tongue e'er told
Lord make me ready for that day
   then Come deare bridgrome Come away.

IV / CONTEMPLATIONS

1

Some time now past in the Autumnal Tide,
When *Phœbus* wanted but one hour to bed,
The trees all richly clad, yet void of pride,
Where gilded o're by his rich golden head.
Their leaves and fruits seem'd painted, but was true
Of green, of red, of yellow, mixed hew,
Rapt were my sences at this delectable view.

2

I wist not what to wish, yet sure thought I,
If so much excellence abide below;
How excellent is he that dwells on high?
Whose power and beauty by his works we know.
Sure he is goodness, wisdome, glory, light,
That hath this under world so richly dight: 13
More Heaven than Earth was here no winter and no
        night.

3

Then on a stately Oak I cast mine Eye,
Whose ruffling top the Clouds seem'd to aspire;
How long since thou wast in thine Infancy?
Thy strength, and stature, more thy years admire,
Hath hundred winters past since thou wast born?
Or thousand since thou brakest thy shell of horn,
If so, all these as nought, Eternity doth scorn.

4

Then higher on the glistering Sun I gaz'd,
Whose beams was shaded by the leavie Tree,
The more I look'd, the more I grew amaz'd,
And softly said, what glory's like to thee?
Soul of this world, this Universes Eye,
No wonder, some made thee a Deity:
Had I not better known, (alas) the same had I.   28

5

Thou as a Bridegroom from thy Chamber rushes,
And as a strong man, joyes to run a race,
The morn doth usher thee, with smiles and blushes,
The Earth reflects her glances in thy face.
Birds, insects, Animals with Vegative,
Thy heat from death and dulness doth revive:
And in the darksome womb of fruitful nature dive.

6

Thy swift Annual, and diurnal Course,
Thy daily streight, and yearly oblique path,
Thy pleasing fervor, and thy scorching force,
All mortals here the feeling knowledg hath.
Thy presence makes it day, thy absence night,
Quaternal Seasons caused by thy might:
Hail Creature, full of sweetness, beauty and delight.   42

7

Art thou so full of glory, that no Eye
Hath strength, thy shining Rayes once to behold?
And is thy splendid Throne erect so high?
As to approach it, can no earthly mould.
How full of glory then must thy Creator be?
Who gave this bright light luster unto thee:
Admir'd, ador'd for ever, be that Majesty.

8

Silent alone, where none or saw, or heard,
In pathless paths I lead my wandring feet,
My humble Eyes to lofty Skyes I rear'd
To sing some Song, my mazed Muse thought meet.
My great Creator I would magnifie,
That nature had, thus decked liberally:
But Ah, and Ah, again, my imbecility!   56

9

I heard the merry grashopper then sing,
The black clad Cricket, bear a second part,
They kept one tune, and plaid on the same string,
Seeming to glory in their little Art.
Shall Creatures abject, thus their voices raise?
And in their kind resound their makers praise:
Whilst I as mute, can warble forth no higher layes.

10

When present times look back to Ages past,
And men in being fancy those are dead,
It makes things gone perpetually to last,
And calls back moneths and years that long since fled
It makes a man more aged in conceit,
Than was *Methuselah*, or's grand-sire great: 69
While of their persons and their acts his mind doth treat.

11

Sometimes in *Eden* fair, he seems to be,
Sees glorious *Adam* there made Lord of all,
Fancyes the Apple, dangle on the Tree,
That turn'd his Sovereign to a naked thral.
Who like a miscreant's driven from that place,
To get his bread with pain, and sweat of face:
A penalty impos'd on his backsliding Race.

12

Here sits our Grandame in retired place,
And in her lap, her bloody *Cain* new born,
The weeping Imp oft looks her in the face,
Bewails his unknown hap, and fate forlorn;
His Mother sighs, to think of Paradise,
And how she lost her bliss, to be more wise,
Believing him that was, and is, Father of lyes.   84

13

Here *Cain* and *Abel* come to sacrifice,
Fruits of the Earth, and Fatlings each do bring,
On *Abels* gift the fire descends from Skies,
But no such sign on false *Cain's* offering;
With sullen hateful looks he goes his wayes.
Hath thousand thoughts to end his brothers dayes,
Upon whose blood his future good he hopes to raise.

14

There *Abel* keeps his sheep, no ill he thinks,
His brother comes, then acts his fratricide,
The Virgin Earth, of blood her first draught drinks
But since that time she often hath been cloy'd;
The wretch with gastly face and dreadful mind,
Thinks each he sees will serve him in his kind,   97
Though none on Earth but kindred near then could he
        find.

15

Who fancyes not his looks now at the Barr,
His face like death, his heart with horror fraught,
Nor Male-factor ever felt like warr,
When deep dispair, with wish of life hath fought,
Branded with guilt, and crusht with treble woes,
A Vagabond to Land of *Nod* he goes.
A City builds, that wals might him secure from foes.

16

Who thinks not oft upon the Fathers ages.
Their long descent, how nephews sons they saw,
The starry observations of those Sages,
And how their precepts to their sons were law,
How Adam sigh'd to see his Progeny,
Cloath'd all in his black sinfull Livery,
Who neither guilt, nor yet the punishment could fly. 112

17

Our Life compare we with their length of dayes
Who to the tenth of theirs doth now arrive?
And though thus short, we shorten many wayes,
Living so little while we are alive;
In eating, drinking, sleeping, vain delight
So unawares comes on perpetual night,
And puts all pleasures vain unto eternal flight.

18

When I behold the heavens as in their prime,
And then the earth (though old) stil clad in green,
The stones and trees, insensible of time,
Nor age nor wrinkle on their front are seen;
If winter come, and greeness then do fade,
A Spring returns, and they more youthfull made;   125
But Man grows old, lies down, remains where once he's
          laid.

19

By birth more noble than those creatures all,
Yet seems by nature and by custome curs'd,
No sooner born, but grief and care makes fall
That state obliterate he had at first:
Nor youth, nor strength, nor wisdom spring again
Nor habitations long their names retain,
But in oblivion to the final day remain.

20

Shall I then praise the heavens, the trees, the earth
Because their beauty and their strength last longer
Shall I wish there, or never to had birth,
Because they're bigger, and their bodyes stronger?
Nay, they shall darken, perish, fade and dye,
And when unmade, so ever shall they lye,
But man was made for endless immortality.   140

21

Under the cooling shadow of a stately Elm
Close sate I by a goodly Rivers side,
Where gliding streams the Rocks did overwhelm;
A lonely place, with pleasures dignifi'd.
I once that lov'd the shady woods so well,
Now thought the rivers did the trees excel,
And if the sun would ever shine, there would I dwell.

22

While on the stealing stream I fixt mine eye,
Which to the long'd for Ocean held its course,
I markt, nor crooks, nor rubs that there did lye
Could hinder ought, but still augment its force:
O happy Flood, quoth I, that holds thy race
Till thou arrive at thy beloved place,
Nor is it rocks or shoals that can obstruct thy pace.   154

23

Nor is't enough, that thou alone may'st slide,
But hundred brooks in thy cleer waves do meet,
So hand in hand along with thee they glide
To *Thetis* house, where all imbrace and greet:
Thou Emblem true, of what I count the best,
O could I lead my Rivolets to rest,
So may we press to that vast mansion, ever blest.

24

Ye Fish which in this liquid Region 'bide,
That for each season, have your habitation,
Now salt, now fresh where you think best to glide
To unknown coasts to give a visitation,
In Lakes and ponds, you leave your numerous fry,
So nature taught, and yet you know not why,
You watry folk that know not your felicity.   168

25

Look how the wantons frisk to tast the air,
Then to the colder bottome streight they dive,
Eftsoon to *Neptun's* glassie Hall repair
To see what trade they great ones there do drive,
Who forrage o're the spacious sea-green field,
And take the trembling prey before it yield,
Whose armour is their scales, their spreading fins their
        shield.

26

While musing thus with contemplation fed,
And thousand fancies buzzing in my brain,
The sweet-tongu'd Philomel percht ore my head,
And chanted forth a most melodious strain
Which rapt me so with wonder and delight,
I judg'd my hearing better than my sight,   181
And wisht me wings with her a while to take my flight.

27

O merry Bird (said I) that fears no snares,
That neither toyles nor hoards up in thy barn,
Feels no sad thoughts, nor cruciating cares
To gain more good, or shun what might thee harm
Thy cloaths ne're wear, thy meat is every where,
Thy bed a bough, thy drink the water cleer,
Reminds not what is past, nor whats to come dost fear.

28

The dawning morn with songs thou dost prevent,
Sets hundred notes unto thy feathered crew,
So each one tunes his pretty instrument,
And warbling out the old, begin anew,
And thus they pass their youth in summer season,
Then follow thee into a better Region,
where winter's never felt by that sweet airy legion.   196

29

Man at the best a creature frail and vain,
In knowledg ignorant, in strength but weak,
Subject to sorrows, losses, sickness, pain,
Each storm his state, his mind, his body break,
From some of these he never finds cessation,
But day or night, within, without, vexation,
Troubles from foes, from friends, from dearest, near'st
Relation.

30

And yet this sinfull creature, frail and vain,
This lump of wretchedness, of sin and sorrow,
This weather-beaten vessel wrackt with pain,
Joyes not in hope of an eternal morrow;
Nor all his losses, crosses and vexation,
In weight, in frequency and long duration   209
Can make him deeply groan for that divine Translation.

31

The Mariner that on smooth waves doth glide,
Sings merrily, and steers his Barque with ease,
As if he had command of wind and tide,
And now become great Master of the seas;
But suddenly a storm spoiles all the sport,
And makes him long for a more quiet port,
Which 'gainst all adverse winds may serve for fort.

32

So he that saileth in this world of pleasure,
Feeding on sweets, that never bit of th' sowre,
That's full of friends, of honour and of treasure,
Fond fool, he takes this earth ev'n for heav'ns bower.
But sad affliction comes and makes him see
Here's neither honour, wealth, nor safety;
Only above is found all with security.   224

33

O Time the fatal wrack of mortal things,
That draws oblivions curtains over kings,
Their sumptuous monuments, men know them not,
Their names without a Record are forgot,
Their parts, their ports, their pomp's all laid in th' dust
Nor wit nor gold, nor buildings scape times rust;
But he whose name is grav'd in the white stone
Shall last and shine when all of these are gone.

V / DIALOGUES AND LAMENTATIONS

The Flesh and the Spirit

In secret place where once I stood
Close by the Banks of *Lacrim* flood
I heard two sisters reason on
Things that are past, and things to come;
One flesh was call'd, who had her eye
On worldly wealth and vanity;
The other Spirit, who did rear
Her thoughts unto a higher sphere:
Sister, quoth Flesh, what liv'st thou on
Nothing but Meditation?   10
Doth Contemplation feed thee so
Regardlesly to let earth goe?
Can Speculation satisfy
Notion without Reality?
Dost dream of things beyond the Moon
And dost thou hope to dwell there soon?
Hast treasures there laid up in store
That all in th' world thou count'st but poor?
Art fancy sick, or turn'd a Sot
To catch at shadowes which are not?   20
Come, come, Ile shew unto thy sence,
Industry hath its recompence.
What canst desire, but thou maist see
True substance in variety?
Dost honour like? acquire the same,
As some to their immortal fame:
And trophyes to thy name erect
Which wearing time shall ne're deject.

For riches dost thou long full sore?
Behold enough of precious store. 30
Earth hath more silver, pearls and gold,
Than eyes can see, or hands can hold.
Affect's thou pleasure? take thy fill,
Earth hath enough of what you will.
Then let not goe, what thou maist find,
For things unknown, only in mind.
Spir. Be still thou unregenerate part,
Disturb no more my setled heart,
For I have vow'd, (and so will doe)
Thee as a foe, still to pursue. 40
And combate with thee will and must,
Untill I see thee laid in th' dust.
Sisters we are, ye twins we be,
Yet deadly feud 'twixt thee and me;
For from one father are we not,
Thou by old Adam wast begot,
But my arise is from above,
Whence my dear father I do love.
Thou speak'st me fair, but hat'st me sore,
Thy flatt'ring shews Ile trust no more. 50
How oft thy slave, hast thou me made,
when I believ'd, what thou hast said,
And never had more cause of woe
Than when I did what thou bad'st doe.
Ile stop mine ears at these thy charms,
And count them for my deadly harms.
Thy sinfull pleasures I doe hate,
Thy riches are to me no bait,
Thine honours doe, nor will I love;
For my ambition lyes above. 60
My greatest honour it shall be
When I am victor over thee,

And triumph shall, with laurel head,
When thou my Captive shalt be led,
How I do live, thou need'st not scoff,
For I have meat thou know'st not off;
The hidden Manna I doe eat,
The word of life it is my meat.
My thoughts do yield me more content
Than can thy hours in pleasure spent.   70
Nor are they shadows which I catch,
Nor fancies vain at which I snatch,
But reach at things that are so high,
Beyond thy dull Capacity;
Eternal substance I do see,
With which inriched I would be:
Mine Eye doth pierce the heavens, and see
What is Invisible to thee.
My garments are not silk nor gold,
Nor such like trash which Earth doth hold,   80
But Royal Robes I shall have on,
More glorious than the glistring Sun;
My Crown not Diamonds, Pearls, and gold,
But such as Angels heads infold.
The City where I hope to dwell,
There's none on Earth can parallel;
The stately Walls both high and strong,
Are made of pretious *Jasper* stone;
The Gates of Pearl, both rich and clear,
And Angels are for Porters there;   90
The Streets thereof transparent gold,
Such as no Eye did e're behold,
A Chrystal River there doth run,
Which doth proceed from the Lambs Throne:
Of Life, there are the waters sure,
Which shall remain for ever pure,

Nor Sun, nor Moon, they have no need,
For glory doth from God proceed:
No Candle there, nor yet Torch light,
For there shall be no darksome night.   100
From sickness and infirmity,
For evermore they shall be free,
Nor withering age shall e're come there,
But beauty shall be bright and clear;
This City pure is not for thee,
For things unclean there shall not be:
If I of Heaven may have my fill,
Take thou the world, and all that will.

The Vanity of all worldly things

As he said vanity, so vain say I,
Oh! vanity, O vain all under Sky;
Where is the man can say, lo I have found
On brittle Earth a Consolation sound?
What is't in honour to be set on high?
No, they like Beasts and Sons of men shall dye:
And whil'st they live, how oft doth turn their fate,
He's now a captive, that was King of late.
What is't in wealth, great Treasures to obtain?
No, that's but labour, anxious care and pain,   10
He heaps up riches, and he heaps up sorrow,
It's his to day, but who's his heir to morrow?
What then? Content in pleasures canst thou find,
More vain than all, that's but to grasp the wind.
The sensual senses for a time they please,
Mean while the conscience rage, who shall appease?
What is't in beauty? No that's but a snare,
They're foul enough to day, that once were fair.

What is't in flowring youth, or manly age?
The first is prone to vice, the last to rage.   20
Where is it then, in wisdom, learning arts?
Sure if on earth, it must be in those parts:
Yet these the wisest man of men did find
But vanity, vexation of mind.
And he that knowes the most, doth still bemoan
He knows not all that here is to be known.
What is it then, to doe as *Stoicks* tell,
Nor laugh, nor weep, let things go ill or well.
Such *Stoicks* are but Stocks such teaching vain,
While man is man, he shall have ease or pain.   30
If not in honour, beauty, age nor treasure,
Nor yet in learning, wisdome, youth nor pleasure,
Where shall I climb, sound, seek, search or find
That *Summum Bonum* which may stay my mind?
There is a path, no vultures eye hath seen,
Where Lion fierce, nor lions whelps have been,
Which leads unto that living Crystal Fount,
Who drinks thereof, the world doth nought account.
The depth and sea have said tis not in me,
With pearl and gold, it shall not valued be.   40
For Saphire, Onix, Topaz who would change:
Its hid from eyes of men, they count it strange.
Death and destruction the fame hath heard,
But where and what it is, from heaven's declar'd,
It brings to honour, which shall ne're decay,
It stores with wealth which time can't wear away.
It yieldeth pleasures far beyond conceit,
And truly beautifies without deceit,
Nor strength, nor wisdome nor fresh youth shall fade
Nor death shall see, but are immortal made.   50
This pearl of price, this tree of life, this spring
Who is possessed of, shall reign a King.

Nor change of state, nor cares shall ever see,
But wear his crown unto eternity:
This satiates the Soul, this stayes the mind,
And all the rest, but Vanity we find.

Davids Lamentation for Saul and Jonathan

2. *Sam*. 1. 19

Alas slain is the Head of Israel,
Illustrious *Saul* whose beauty did excell,
Upon thy places mountainous and high,
How did the Mighty fall, and falling dye?
In *Gath* let not this thing be spoken on,
Nor published in streets of *Askalon*,
Lest daughters of the Philistines rejoyce,
Lest the uncircumcis'd lift up their voice.
O *Gilbo* Mounts, let never pearled dew,
Nor fruitfull showres your barren tops bestrew,   10
Nor fields of offrings ever on you grow,
Nor any pleasant thing e're may you show;
For there the Mighty Ones did soon decay,
The shield of *Saul* was vilely cast away,
There had his dignity so sore a foyle,
As if his head ne're felt the sacred oyle.
Sometimes from crimson, blood of gastly slain,
The bow of *Jonathan* ne're turn'd in vain:
Nor from the fat, and spoils of Mighty men
With bloodless sword did *Saul* turn back agen.   20
Pleasant and lovely, were they both in life,
And in their death was found no parting strife.
Swifter than swiftest Eagles so were they,
Stronger than Lions ramping for their prey.

O Israels Dames, o'reflow your beauteous eyes
For valiant *Saul* who on Mount *Gilbo* lyes,
Who cloathed you in Cloath of richest Dye,
And choice delights, full of variety,
On your array put ornaments of gold,
Which made you yet more beauteous to behold.   30
O! how in Battle did the mighty fall
In midst of strength not succoured at ali.
O lovely *Jonathan*! how wast thou slain?
In places high, full low thou didst remain.
Distrest for thee I am, dear *Jonathan*,
Thy love was wonderfull, surpassing man,
Exceeding all the love that's Feminine,
So pleasant hast thou been, dear brother mine:
How are the mighty fall'n into decay,
And warlike weapons perished away.   40

*A Dialogue between Old England and New; concerning
their present Troubles, Anno, 1642*

New-England

Alas dear Mother, fairest Queen and best,
With honour, wealth, and peace, happy and blest;
What ails thee hang thy head, and cross thine arms?
And sit i'th' dust, to sigh these sad alarms?
What deluge of new woes thus over-whelme
The glories of thy ever famous Realme?
What means this wailing tone, this mournful guise?
Ah, tell thy daughter, she may sympathize.

Old England

Art ignorant indeed of these my woes?
Or must my forced tongue these griefs disclose?   10

And must myself dissect my tatter'd state,
Which 'mazed Christendome stands wondring at?
And thou a Child, a Limbe, and dost not feel
My fainting weakned body now to reel?
This Physick purging potion, I have taken,
Will bring consumption, or an Ague quaking,
Unless some Cordial, thou fetch from high,
Which present help may ease my malady.
If I decease, dost think thou shalt survive?
Or by my wasting state dost think to thrive?   20
Then weigh our case, if't be not justly sad;
Let me lament alone, while thou art glad.

New-England

And thus (alas) your state you much deplore
In general terms, but will not say wherefore:
What medicine shall I seek to cure this woe,
If th' wound's so dangerous I may not know.
But you perhaps, would have me ghess it out:
What hath some *Hengist* like that *Saxon* stout
By fraud or force usurp'd thy flowring crown,
Or by tempestuous warrs thy fields trod down?   30
Or hath *Canutus*, that brave valiant *Dane*
The Regal peacefull Scepter from thee tane?
Or is't a *Norman*, whose victorious hand
With English blood bedews thy conquered land?
Or is't Intestine warrs that thus offend?
Do *Maud* and *Stephen* for the crown contend?
Do Barons rise and side against their King,
And call in foraign aid to help the thing?
Must *Edward* be depos'd? or is't the hour
That second *Richard* must be clapt i'th tower?   40
Or is't the fatal jarre, again begun

That from the red white pricking roses sprung?
Must *Richmonds* aid, the Nobles now implore?
To come and break the Tushes of the Boar,
If none of these dear Mother, what's your woe?
Pray do you fear *Spains* bragging *Armado*?
Doth your Allye, fair *France*, conspire your wrack,
Or do the *Scots* play false, behind your back?
Doth *Holland* quit you ill for all your love?
Whence is the storm from Earth or Heaven above?   50
Is't drought, is't famine, or is't pestilence?
Dost feel the smart, or fear the Consequence?
Your humble Child intreats you, shew your grief,
Though Arms, nor Purse she hath for your relief,
Such is her poverty: yet shall be found
A Suppliant for your help, as she is bound.

Old England

I must confess some of those sores you name,
My beauteous body at this present maime;
But forreign foe, nor feigned friend I fear,   59
For they have work enough (thou knowst) elsewhere
Nor is it *Alcies* Son, nor *Henryes* daughter;
Whose proud contention cause this slaughter,
Nor Nobles siding, to make *John* no King,
French Lewis unjustly to the Crown to bring;
No *Edward*, *Richard*, to lose rule and life,
Nor no *Lancastrians* to renew old strife:
No Duke of *York*, nor Earl of *March* to soyle
Their hands in kindreds blood whom they did foil
No crafty Tyrant now usurps the Seat,
Who Nephews slew that so he might be great;   70
No need of *Tudor*, Roses to unite,
None knows which is the red, or which the white;

Spains braving Fleet, a second time is sunk,
France knows how oft my fury she hath drunk:
By *Edward* third, and *Henry* fifth of fame,
Her Lillies in mine Arms avouch the same.
My Sister *Scotland* hurts me now no more,
Though she hath been injurious heretofore;
What *Holland* is I am in some suspence?
But trust not much unto his excellence.   80
For wants, sure some I feel, but more I fear,
And for the Pestilence, who knows how near;
Famine and Plague, two Sisters of the Sword,
Destruction to a Land, doth soon afford:
They're for my punishment ordain'd on high,
Unless our tears prevent it speedily.
But yet I Answer not what you demand,
To shew the grievance of my troubled Land?
Before I tell th' Effect, I'le shew the Cause
Which are my sins the breach of sacred Laws,   90
Idolatry supplanter of a Nation,
With foolish Superstitious Adoration,
Are lik'd and countenanc'd by men of might,
The Gospel troden down and hath no right:
Church Offices were sold and bought for gain,
That Pope had hope to find, *Rome* here again,
For Oaths and Blasphemies, did ever Ear,
From *Belzebub* himself such language hear;
What scorning of the Saints of the most high?
What injuries did daily on them lye?   100
What false reports, what nick-names did they take
Not for their own, but for their Masters sake?
And thou poor soul, wert jeer'd among the rest,
Thy flying for the truth was made a jest.
For Sabbath-breaking, and for drunkenness,
Did ever land profaness more express?

From crying blood yet cleansed am not I,
Martyres and others, dying causelesly.
How many princely heads on blocks laid down
For nought but title to a fading crown?   110
'Mongst all the crueltyes by great ones done
Oh *Edwards* youths, and *Clarence* hapless son,
O *Jane* why didst thou dye in flowring prime?
Because of royal stem, that was thy crime.
For bribery Adultery and lyes,
Where is the nation, I can't parallize.
With usury, extortion and oppression,
These be the *Hydraes* of my stout transgression.
These be the bitter fountains, heads and roots,   119
Whence flow'd the source, the sprigs, the boughs and fruits
Of more than thou canst hear or I relate,
That with high hand I still did perpetrate:
For these were threatned the wofull day,
I mockt the Preachers, put it far away;
The Sermons yet upon Record do stand
That cri'd destruction to my wicked land:
I then believ'd not, now I feel and see,
The plague of stubborn incredulity.
Some lost their livings, some in prison pent,
Some fin'd, from house and friends to exile went.   130
Their silent tongues to heaven did vengeance cry,
Who saw their wrongs, and hath judg'd righteously
And will repay it seven-fold in my lap:
This is fore-runner of my Afterclap.
Nor took I warning by my neighbours falls,
I saw sad *Germanyes* dismantled walls,
I saw her people famish'd, Nobles slain,
Her fruitfull land, a barren Heath remain.
I saw unmov'd, her Armyes foil'd and fled,
Wives forc'd, babes toss'd, her houses calcined.   140

I saw strong *Rochel* yielded to her Foe,
Thousands of starved Christians there also.
I saw poor *Ireland* bleeding out her last,
Such crueltyes as all reports have past;
Mine heart obdurate stood not yet agast.
Now sip I of that cup, and just't may be
The bottome dreggs reserved are for me.

New-England

To all you've said, sad Mother I assent,
Your fearfull sins great cause there's to lament,
My guilty hands in part, hold up with you,   150
A Sharer in your punishment's my due.
But all you say amounts to this effect,
Not what you feel, but what you do expect,
Pray in plain terms, what is your present grief?
Then let's joyn heads and hearts for your relief.

Old England

Well to the matter then, there's grown of late
'Twixt King and Peers a Question of State,
Which is the chief, the Law, or else the King.
One said, it's he, the other no such thing.
'Tis said, my beter part in Parliament   160
To ease my groaning Land, shew'd their intent,
To crush the proud, and right to each man deal,
To help the Church, and stay the Common-weal.
So many Obstacles came in their way,
As puts me to a stand what I should say;
Old customes, new Prerogatives stood on,
Had they not held Law fast, all had been gone:

Which by their prudence stood them in such stead
They took high *Strafford* lower by the head.
And to their *Laud* be't spoke, they held i'th tower   170
All *Englands* Metropolitane that hour;
This done, an act they would have passed fain,
No Prelate should his Bishoprick retain;
Here tugg'd they hard (indeed,) for all men saw
This must be done by Gospel, not by Law.
Next the Militia they urged sore,
This was deny'd, (I need not say wherefore)
The King displeas'd at *York*, himself absents,
They humbly beg return, shew their intents;
The writing, printing, posting too and fro,   180
Shews all was done, I'le therefore let it go.
But now I come to speak of my disaster,
Contention grown, 'twixt Subjects and their Master;
They worded it so long, they fell to blows,
That thousands lay on heaps, here bleeds my woes,
I that no wars so many years have known,
Am now destroy'd and slaught'red by mine own;
But could the Field alone this strife decide,
One Battel two or three I might abide:
But these may be beginnings of more woe   190
Who knows, but this may be my overthrow.
Oh pity me in this sad perturbation,
My plundred Towns, my houses devastation,
My weeping Virgins and my young men slain;
My wealthy trading fall'n, my dearth of grain,
The seed-times come, but ploughman hath no hope
Because he knows not who shall inn his Crop:
The poor they want their pay, their children bread,
Their woful Mothers tears unpittied,
If any pity in thy heart remain,   200
Or any child-like love thou dost retain,

For my relief, do what there lyes in thee,
And recompence that good I've done to thee.

New England

Dear Mother cease complaints and wipe your eyes,
Shake off your dust, chear up, and now arise,
You are my Mother Nurse, and I your flesh,
Your sunken bowels gladly would refresh,
Your griefs I pity, but soon hope to see,
Out of your troubles much good fruit to be;
To see those latter dayes of hop'd for good,   210
Though now beclouded all with tears and blood:
After dark Popery the day did clear,
But now the Sun in's brightness shall appear.
Blest be the Nobles of thy noble Land,
With ventur'd lives for Truths defence that stand.
Blest be thy Commons, who for common good,
And thy infringed Laws have boldly stood.
Blest be thy Counties, who did aid thee still,
With hearts and States to testifie their will.
Blest be thy Preachers, who do chear thee on,   220
O cry the Sword of God, and *Gideon*;
And shall I not on them wish *Mero*'s curse,
That help thee not with prayers, Arms and purse?
And for my self let miseries abound,
If mindless of thy State I e're be found.
These are the dayes the Churches foes to crush,
To root out Popelings head, tail, branch and rush;
Let's bring *Baals* vestments forth to make a fire,
Their Mytires, Surplices, and all their Tire,
Copes, Rotchets, Crossiers, and such empty trash,   230
And let their Names consume, but let the flash
Light Christendome, and all the world to see
We hate *Romes* whore, with all her trumpery.

Go on brave *Essex* with a Loyal heart,
Not false to King, nor to the better part;
But those that hurt his people and his Crown,
As duty binds, expel and tread them down.
And ye brave Nobles chase away all fear,
And to this hopeful Cause closely adhere;
O Mother can you weep, and have such Peers,   240
When they are gone, then drown your self in tears
If now you weep so much, that then no more
The briny Ocean will o'reflow your shore.
These, these are they I trust, with *Charles* our King,
Out of all mists such glorious dayes shall bring;
That dazled eyes beholding much shall wonder
At that thy setled peace, thy wealth and splendor.
Thy Church and weal establish'd in such manner,
That all shall joy, that thou display'dst thy Banner;
And discipline erected so I trust,   250
That nursing Kings shall come and lick thy dust:
Then Justice shall in all thy Courts take place,
Without respect of person, or of case;
Then Bribes shall cease, and Suits shall not stick long
Patience and purse of Clients oft to wrong:
Then high Commissions shall fall to decay,
And pursivants, and Catchpoles want their pay.
So shall thy happy Nation ever flourish,
When truth and righteousnes they thus shall nourish;
When thus in peace, thine Armies brave send out,   260
To sack proud *Rome*, and all her Vassals rout;
There let thy Name, thy fame, and glory shine,
As did thine Ancestors in *Palestine*:
And let her spoyls full pay, with Interest be,
Of what unjustly once she poll'd from thee.
Of all the woes thou canst, let her be sped,
And on her pour the vengeance threatned;

Bring forth the Beast that rul'd the World with's beck,
And tear his flesh, and set your feet on's neck;
And make his filthy Den so desolate,   270
To th' stonishment of all that knew his state:
This done with brandish'd Swords to *Turky* goe,
For then what is't, but English blades dare do,
And lay her waste for so's the sacred Doom,
And do to *Gog* as thou hast done to *Rome*.
Oh *Abraham*'s seed lift up your heads on high,
For sure the day of your Redemption's nigh;
The Scales shall fall from your long blinded eyes,
And him you shall adore who now despise,
Then fulness of the Nations in shall flow,   280
And Jew and Gentile to one worship go;
Then follows dayes of happiness and rest;
Whose lot doth fall, to live therein is blest:
No Canaanite shall then be found i'th' Land,
And holiness on horses bells shall stand.
If this make way thereto, then sigh no more,
But if at all, thou didst not see't before;
Farewel dear Mother, rightest cause prevail,
And in a while, you'le tell another tale.

VI / FORMAL ELEGIES

*In Honour of that High and Mighty Princess
Queen Elizabeth of happy memory*

The Proeme

Although great Queen thou now in silence lye
Yet thy loud Herald Fame doth to the sky
Thy wondrous worth proclaim in every Clime,
And so hath vow'd while there is world or time.
So great's thy glory and thine excellence,
The sound thereof rapts every humane sence,
That men account it no impiety,
To say thou wert a fleshly Diety:
Thousands bring offerings (though out of date)
Thy world of honours to accumulate,   10
'Mongst hundred Hecatombs of roaring verse,
Mine bleating stands before thy royal Herse.
Thou never didst nor canst thou now disdain
T' accept the tribute of a loyal brain.
Thy clemency did yerst esteem as much
The acclamations of the poor as rich,
Which makes me deem my rudeness is no wrong,
Though I resound thy praises 'mongst the throng.

The Poem

No *Phœnix* pen, nor *Spencers* poetry,
No *Speeds* nor *Cambdens* learned History,   20
*Elizah*s works, warrs, praise, can e're compact,
The World's the Theatre where she did act.
No memoryes nor volumes can contain
The 'leven Olympiads of her happy reign:

Who was so good, so just, so learn'd so wise,
From all the Kings on earth she won the prize.
Nor say I more than duly is her due,
Millions will testifie that this is true.
She hath wip'd off th' aspersion of her Sex,
That women wisdome lack to play the Rex: 30
Spains Monarch, sayes not so, nor yet his host:
She taught them better manners, to their cost.
The *Salique* law, in force now had not been,
If *France* had ever hop'd for such a Queen.
But can you Doctors now this point dispute,
She's Argument enough to make you mute.
Since first the sun did run his nere run race,
And earth had once a year, a new old face,
Since time was time, and man unmanly man,
Come shew me such a *Phœnix* if you can?   40
Was ever people better rul'd than hers?
Was ever land more happy freed from stirrs?
Did ever wealth in *England* more abound?
Her victoryes in forreign Coasts resound,
Ships more invincible than *Spain*'s, her foe
She wrackt, she sackt, she sunk his Armado:
Her stately troops advanc'd to *Lisbons* wall
Don Anthony in's right there to install.
She frankly helpt, *Franks* brave distressed King,
The States united now her fame do sing,   50
She their Protectrix was, they well do know
Unto our dread Virago, what they owe.
Her Nobles sacrific'd their noble blood,
Nor men nor Coyn she spar'd to do them good.
The rude untamed *Irish*, she did quel,
Before her picture the proud *Tyrone* fell.
Had ever prince such Counsellours as she?
Her self *Minerva* caus'd them so to be.

Such Captains and such souldiers never seen,
As were the Subjects of our *Pallas* Queen.   60
Her Sea-men through all straights the world did round;
Terra incognita might know the sound.
Her *Drake* came laden home with Spanish gold:
Her *Essex* took *Cades*, their Herculean Hold:
But time would fail me, so my tongue would to,
To tell of half she did, or she could doe.
Semiramis to her, is but obscure,
More infamy than fame, she did procure.
She built her glory but on *Babels* walls,
Worlds wonder for a while, but yet it falls.   70
Fierce *Tomris*, (*Cyrus* heads-man) *Scythians* queen,
Had put her harness off, had shee but seen
Our Amazon in th' Camp of *Tilbury*,
Judging all valour and all Majesty
Within that Princess to have residence,
And prostrate yielded to her excellence.
Dido first Foundress of proud *Carthage* walls,
(Who living consummates her Funeralls)
A great *Eliza*, but compar'd with ours,
How vanisheth her glory, wealth and powers.   80
Profuse, proud *Cleopatra*, whose wrong name,
Instead of glory, prov'd her Countryes shame:
Of her what worth in Storyes to be seen,
But that she was a rich Egyptian Queen.
Zenobya potent Empress of the East,
And of all these, without compare the best,
Whom none but great *Aurelius* could quel;
Yet for our Queen is no fit Parallel.
She was a Phœnix Queen, so shall she be,
Her ashes not reviv'd, more Phœnix she.   90
Her personal perfections, who would tell,
Must dip his pen in th' *Heleconian Well*,

Which I may not, my pride doth but aspire
To read what others write, and so admire.
Now say, have women worth? or have they none?
Or had they some, but with our Queen is't gone?
Nay Masculines, you have thus taxt us long,
But she, though dead, will vindicate our wrong.
Let such as say our Sex is void of Reason,
Know tis a Slander now, but once was Treason.   100
But happy *England* which had such a Queen;
Yea happy, happy, had those dayes still been:
But happiness lyes in a higher sphere,
Then wonder not *Eliza* moves not here.
Full fraught with honour, riches and with dayes
She set, she set, like *Titan* in his rayes.
No more shall rise or set so glorious sun
Untill the heavens great revolution,
If then new things their old forms shall retain,
Eliza shall rule *Albion* once again.   110

Her Epitaph

Here sleeps the Queen, this is the Royal Bed,
Of th' Damask Rose, sprung from the white and red,
Whose sweet perfume fills the all-filling Air:
This Rose is wither'd, once so lovely fair.
On neither tree did grow such Rose before,
The greater was our gain, our loss the more.

Another

Here lyes the pride of Queens, Pattern of Kings,
So blaze it Fame, here's feathers for thy wings.
Here lyes the envi'd, yet unparalled Prince,
Whose living virtues speak, (though dead long since)   120
If many worlds, as that Fantastick fram'd,
In every one be her great glory fam'd.

An Elegie upon that Honourable and renowned Knight Sir Philip Sidney, who was untimely slain at the Siege of Zutphen, Anno, 1586

When *England* did enjoy her Halsion dayes,
Her noble *Sidney* wore the Crown of Bayes;
As well an honour to our *British* Land,
As she that sway'd the Scepter with her hand;
Mars and *Minerva* did in one agree,
Of Arms and Arts he should a pattern be,
Calliope with *Terpsichore* did sing,
Of Poesie, and of musick, he was King;
His Rhetorick struck *Polimina* dead,
His Eloquence made *Mercury* wax red;   10
His *Logick* from *Euterpe* won the Crown,
More worth was his than *Clio* could set down.
Thalia and *Melpomene* say truth,
(Witness *Arcadia* penned in his youth,)
Are not his tragick Comedies so acted,
As if your ninefold wit had been compacted.
To shew the world, they never saw before,
That this one Volume should exhaust your store;
His wiser dayes condemn'd his witty works,
Who knows the spels that in his Rhetorick lurks,   20
But some infatuate fools soon caught therein,
Fond *Cupids* Dame had never such a gin,
Which makes severer eyes but slight that story,
And men of morose minds envy his glory:
But he's a Beetle-head that can't descry
A world of wealth within that rubbish lye,
And doth his name, his work, his honour wrong,
The brave refiner of our British tongue,
That sees not learning, valour and morality,
Justice, friendship, and kind hospitality,   30

Yea and Divinity within his book,
Such were prejudicate, and did not look.
In all Records his name I ever see
Put with an Epithite of dignity,
Which shews his worth was great, his honour such,
The love his Country ought him, was as much.
Then let none disallow of these my straines
Whilst English blood yet runs within my veins.
O brave *Achilles*, I wish some *Homer* would
Engrave in Marble, with Characters of gold   40
The valiant feats thou didst on *Flanders* coast,
Which at this day fair *Belgia* may boast.
The more I say, the more thy worth I stain,
Thy fame and praise is far beyond my strain.
O *Zutphen*, *Zutphen* that most fatal City
Made famous by thy death, much more the pity:
Ah! in his blooming prime death pluckt this rose
E're he was ripe, his thread cut *Atropos*.
Thus man is born to dye, and dead is he,
Brave *Hector*, by the walls of *Troy* we see.   50
O who was near thee but did sore repine
He rescued not with life that life of thine:
But yet impartial Fates this boon did give,
Though *Sidney* di'd his valiant name should live:
And live it doth in spight of death through fame,
Thus being overcome, he overcame.
Where is that envious tongue, but can afford
Of this our noble *Scipio* some good word.
Great *Bartas* this unto thy praise adds more,
In sad sweet verse, thou didst his death deplore.   60
And *Phœnix Spencer* doth unto his life,
His death present in sable to his wife.
Stella the fair, whose streams from Conduits fell
For the sad loss of her dear *Astrophel*.

Fain would I shew how he fames paths did tread,
But now into such Lab'rinths I am lead,
With endless turnes, the way I find not out,
How to persist my Muse is more in doubt;
Which makes me now with *Silvester* confess,
But *Sidney*'s Muse can sing his worthiness.   70
The Muses aid I crav'd, they had no will
To give to their Detractor any quill,
With high disdain, they said they gave no more,
Since *Sidney* had exhausted all their store.
They took from me the scribling pen I had,
(I to be eas'd of such a task was glad)
Then to reveng this wrong, themselves engage,
And drave me from *Parnassus* in a rage.
Then wonder not if I no better sped,
Since I the Muses thus have injured.   80
I pensive for my fault, sate down, and then
Errata through their leave, threw me my pen,
My Poem to conclude, two lines they deign
Which writ, she bad return't to them again;
So *Sidneys* fame I leave to *Englands* Rolls,
His bones do lie interr'd in stately *Pauls*.

His Epitaph

Here lies in fame under this stone,
Philip and *Alexander* both in one;
Heir to the Muses, the Son of *Mars* in Truth,
Learning, Valour, Wisdome, all in virtuous youth,   90
His praise is much, this shall suffice my pen,
That *Sidney* dy'd 'mong most renown'd of men.

In honour of Du Bartas, 1641

Among the happy wits this age hath shown,
Great, dear, sweet *Bartas* thou art matchless known;
My ravish'd Eyes and heart with faltering tongue,
In humble wise have vow'd their service long,
But knowing th' task so great, and strength but small,
Gave o're the work before begun withal,
My dazled sight of late review'd thy lines,
Where Art, and more than Art, in nature shines,
Reflection from their beaming Altitude,
Did thaw my frozen hearts ingratitude;   10
Which Rayes darting upon some richer ground,
Had caused flours and fruits soon to abound;
But barren I my Dasey here do bring,
A homely flour in this my latter Spring,
If summer, or my Autumn age do yield,
Flours, fruits, in Garden, Orchard, or in Field,
They shall be consecrated in my Verse,
And prostrate offered at great *Bartas* Herse;
My muse unto a Child I may compare,
Who sees the riches of some famous Fair,   20
He feeds his Eyes, but understanding lacks
To comprehend the worth of all those knacks:
The glittering plate and Jewels he admires,
The Hats and Fans, the Plumes and Ladies tires,
And thousand times his mazed mind doth wish
Some part (at least) of that brave wealth was his,
But seeing empty wishes nought obtain,
At night turns to his Mothers cot again,
And tells her tales, (his full heart over glad)
Of all the glorious sights his Eyes have had: 30
But finds too soon his want of Eloquence,
The silly pratler speaks no word of sense;

But seeing utterance fail his great desires,
Sits down in silence, deeply he admires:
Thus weak brain'd I, reading thy lofty stile,
Thy profound learning, viewing other while;
Thy Art in natural Philosophy,
Thy Saint like mind in grave Divinity;
Thy piercing skill in high Astronomy,
And curious insight in Anatomy: 40
Thy Physick, musick and state policy,
Valour in warr, in peace good husbandry.
Sure lib'ral Nature did with Art not small,
In all the arts make thee most liberal.
A thousand thousand times my sensless sences
Moveless stand charm'd by thy sweet influences;
More sensless than the stones to *Amphions* Lute,
Mine eyes are sightless, and my tongue is mute,
My full astonish'd heart doth pant to break,
Through grief it wants a faculty to speak: 50
Volleyes of praises could I eccho then,
Had I an Angels voice, or *Bartas* pen:
But wishes can't accomplish my desire,
Pardon if I adore, when I admire.
O France thou did'st in him more glory gain
Than in thy *Martel*, *Pipin*, *Charlemain*,
Than in St. *Lewes*, or thy last *Henry* Great,
Who tam'd his foes in warrs, in bloud and sweat.
Thy fame is spread as far, I dare be bold,
In all the Zones, the temp'rate, hot and cold.   60
Their Trophies were but heaps of wounded slain,
Thine, the quintessence of an heroick brain.
The oaken Garland ought to deck their brows,
Immortal Bayes to thee all men allows.
Who in thy tryumphs never won by wrongs,
Lead'st millions chaind by eyes, by ears, by tongues.

Oft have I wondred at the hand of heaven,
In giving one what would have served seven.
If e're this golden gift was showr'd on any,
Thy double portion would have served many.   70
Unto each man his riches is assign'd
Of Name, of State, of Body and of Mind:
Thou hadst thy part of all, but of the last,
O pregnant brain, O comprehension vast:
Thy haughty Stile and rapted wit sublime
All ages wondring at, shall never climb.
Thy sacred works are not for imitation,
But Monuments to future Admiration.
Thus *Bartas* fame shall last while starrs do stand,
And whilst there's Air or Fire, or Sea or Land.   80
But least mine ignorance should do thee wrong,
To celebrate thy merits in my Song,
I'le leave thy praise to those shall do thee right,
Good will, not skill, did cause me bring my Mite.

His Epitaph

Here lyes the Pearle of France, Parnassus *Glory;*
The World rejoyc'd at's birth, at's death was sorry.
Art and Nature joyn'd, by heavens high decree
Now shew'd what once they ought, Humanity:
And Natures Law, had it been revocable
To rescue him from death, Art had been able.   90
But Nature vanquish'd Art, so Bartas *dy'd;*
But Fame out-living both, he is reviv'd.

Part Two

LONGER POEMS

THE
TENTH MUSE

Lately ſprung up in AMERICA.

OR

Severall Poems, compiled

with great variety of VVit
and Learning, full of delight.
Wherein eſpecially is contained a com-
pleat diſcourſe and deſcription of

The Four {
Elements,
Conſtitutions,
Ages of Man,
Seaſons of the Year.

Together with an Exact Epitomie of
the Four Monarchies, *viz.*

The {
Aſſyrian,
Perſian,
Grecian,
Roman.

Alſo a Dialogue between Old *England* and
New, concerning the late troubles.
With divers other pleaſant and ſerious Poems.

By a Gentlewoman in thoſe parts.

Printed at London for *Stephen Bowtell* at the ſigne of the
Bible in Popes Head-Alley. 1650.

Title page of The Tenth Muse . . ., *London, 1650.*

*To her most Honoured Father Thomas Dudley Esq;
these humbly presented*

Dear Sir of late delighted with the sight
Of your four Sisters cloth'd in black and white,
Of fairer Dames the Sun, ne'r saw the face;
Though made a pedestal for *Adams* Race;
Their worth so shines in these rich lines you show
Their paralels to finde I scarcely know
To climbe their Climes, I have nor strength nor skill
To mount so high requires an Eagles quill;
Yet view thereof did cause my thoughts to soar;
My lowly pen might wait upon these four,   10
I bring my four times four, now meanly clad
To do their homage, unto yours, full glad:
Who for their Age, their worth and quality
Might seem of yours to claim precedency:
But by my humble hand, thus rudely pen'd
They are, your bounden handmaids to attend.
These same are they, from whom we being have,
These are of all, the Life, the Nurse, the Grave,
These are the hot, the cold, the moist, the dry,
That sink, that swim, that fill, that upwards fly,   20
Of these consists our bodies, Cloathes and Food,
The World, the useful, hurtful, and the good,
Sweet harmony they keep, yet jar oft times
Their discord doth appear, by these harsh rimes.
Yours did contest for wealth, for Arts, for Age,
My first do shew their good, and then their rage.
My other foures do intermixed tell
Each others faults, and where themselves excell;
How hot and dry contend with moist and cold,
How Air and Earth no correspondence hold,   30

And yet in equal tempers, how they 'gree
How divers natures make one Unity
Something of all (though mean) I did intend
But fear'd you'ld judge *Du Bartas* was my friend,
I honour him, but dare not wear his wealth
My goods are true (though poor) I love no stealth
But if I did I durst not send them you
Who must reward a Thief, but with his due.
I shall not need, mine innocence to clear
These ragged lines, will do't, when they appear: 40
On what they are, your mild aspect I crave
Accept my best, my worst vouchsafe a Grave.

From her that to your self, more duty owes
Than water in the boundlesse Ocean flows.

The Prologue

1

To sing of Wars, of Captains, and of Kings,
Of Cities founded, Common-wealths begun,
For my mean pen are too superiour things:
Or how they all, or each their dates have run
Let Poets and Historians set these forth,   5
My obscure Lines shall not so dim their worth.

2

But when my wondring eyes and envious heart
Great *Bartas* sugar'd lines, do but read o're
Fool I do grudg the Muses did not part
'Twixt him and me that overfluent store;   10
A *Bartas* can, do what a *Bartas* will
But simple I according to my skill.   12

3

From school-boyes tongue no rhet'rick we expect
Nor yet a sweet Consort from broken strings,
Nor perfect beauty, where's a main defect:
My foolish, broken, blemish'd Muse so sings
And this to mend, alas, no Art is able,
'Cause nature, made it so irreparable.

4

Nor can I, like that fluent sweet tongu'd Greek,
Who lisp'd at first, in future times speak plain
By Art he gladly found what he did seek
A full requital of his striving paine:
Art can do much, but this maxime's most sure
A weak or wounded brain admits no cure.

5

I am obnoxious to each carping tongue
Who says my hand a needle better fits,
A Poets pen all scorn I should thus wrong,
For such despite they cast on Female wits:
If what I do prove well, it won't advance,
They'l say it's stoln, or else it was by chance.

6

But sure the Antique Greeks were far more mild
Else of our Sexe, why feigned they those Nine
And poesy made, *Calliope's* own Child;
So 'mongst the rest they placed the Arts Divine,
But this weak knot, they will full soon untie,
The Greeks did nought, but play the fools and lye.   36

7

Let Greeks be Greeks, and women what they are
Men have precedency and still excell,
It is but vain unjustly to wage warre;
Men can do best, and women know it well
Preheminence in all and each is yours;
Yet grant some small acknowledgement of ours.

8

And oh ye high flown quills that soar the Skies,
And ever with your prey still catch your praise,
If e're you daigne these lowly lines your eyes
Give Thyme or Parsley wreath, I ask no bayes,
This mean and unrefined ure of mine
Will make your glistering gold but more to shine.   48

The Four Elements

The Fire, Air, Earth and water did contest
Which was the strongest, noblest and the best,
Who was of greatest use and might'est force;
In placide Terms they thought now to discourse,
That in due order each her turn should speak;
But enmity this amity did break
All would be chief, and all scorn'd to be under
Whence issu'd winds and rains, lightning and thunder
The quaking earth did groan, the Sky lookt black
The Fire, the forced Air, in sunder crack;   10
The sea did threat the heav'ns, the heavn's the earth,
All looked like a Chaos or new birth:

Fire broyled Earth, and scorched Earth it choaked
Both by their darings, water so provoked
That roaring in it came, and with its source
Soon made the Combatants abate their force,
The rumbling hissing, puffing was so great
The worlds confusion, it did seem to threat
Till gentle Air, Contention so abated
That betwixt hot and cold, she arbitrated   20
The others difference, being less did cease
All storms now laid, and they in perfect peace
That Fire should first begin, the rest consent,
The noblest and most active Element.

    Fire

What is my worth (both ye) and all men know,
In little time I can but little show,
But what I am, let learned Grecians say
What I can do well skil'd Mechanicks may:
The benefit all living by me finde,
All sorts of Artists, here declare your mind,   30
What tool was ever fram'd, but by my might?
Ye Martilists, what weapons for your fight
To try your valour by, but it must feel
My force? your sword, and Gun, your Lance of steel
Your Cannon's bootless and your powder too
Without mine aid, (alas) what can they do:
The adverse walls not shak'd, the Mines not blown
And in despight the City keeps her own;
But I with one Granado or Petard
Set ope those gates, that 'fore so strong were barr'd.   40
Ye Husband-men, your Coulters made by me
Your Hooes your Mattocks, and what e're you see
Subdue the Earth, and fit it for your Grain
That so it might in time requite your pain:

Though strong limb'd Vulcan forg'd it by his skill
I made it flexible unto his will;
Ye Cooks, your Kitchen implements I frame
Your Spits, Pots, Jacks, what else I need not name
Your dayly food I wholsome make, I warm   49
Your shrinking Limbs, which winter's cold doth harm
Ye *Paracelsians* too in vain's your skill
In Chymistry, unless I help you Still.
And you Philosophers, if e're you made
A transmutation it was through mine aid.
Ye silver Smiths, your Ure I do refine
What mingled lay with Earth I cause to shine;
But let me leave these things, my flame aspires
To match on high with the Celestial fires:
The Sun an Orb of fire was held of old,
Our Sages new another tale have told: 60
But be he what they will, yet his aspect
A burning fiery heat we find reflect
And of the self same nature is with mine
Cold sister Earth, no witness needs but thine:
How doth his warmth, refresh thy frozen back
And trim thee brave, in green, after thy black.
Both man and beast rejoyce at his approach,
And birds do sing, to see his glittering Coach
And though nought, but *Salmanders* live in fire
And fly Pyrausta call'd, all else expire,   70
Yet men and beasts Astronomers will tell
Fixed in heavenly Constellations dwell,
My Planets of both Sexes whose degree
Poor Heathen judg'd worthy a Diety:
There's *Orion* arm'd attended by his dog;
The *Theban* stout *Alcides* with his Club;
The valiant *Perseus*, who *Medusa* slew,
The horse that kil'd *Belerophon*, then flew.

My Crab, my Scorpion, fishes you may see
The Maid with ballance, wain with horses three,   80
The Ram, the Bull, the Lion, and the Beagle,
The Bear, the Goat, the Raven, and the Eagle,
The Crown the Whale, the Archer, Bernice Hare
The Hidra, Dolphin, Boys that water bear,
Nay more, than these, Rivers 'mongst stars are found
Eridanus, where *Phaeton* was drown'd.
Their magnitude, and height, should I recount
My story to a volume would amount;
Out of a multitude these few I touch,
Your wisdome out of little gather much.   90
I'le here let pass, my choler, cause of wars
And influence of divers of those stars
When in Conjunction with the Sun do more
Augment his heat, which was too hot before.
The Summer ripening season I do claim
And man from thirty unto fifty frame.
Of old when Sacrifices were Divine,
I of acceptance was the holy signe,
'Mong all my wonders which I might recount,   99
There's none more strange than *Ætna*'s Sulphry mount
The choaking flames, that from *Vesuvius* flew
The over curious second *Pliny* slew,
And with the Ashes that it sometimes shed
Apulia's 'jacent parts were covered.
And though I be a servant to each man
Yet by my force, master, my masters can.
What famous Towns, to Cinders have I turn'd?
What lasting forts my kindled wrath hath burn'd?
The stately Seats of mighty Kings by me
In confused heaps, of ashes may you see.   110
Wher's *Ninus* great wall'd Town, and *Troy* of old
Carthage, and hundred more in stories told

Which when they could not be o'recome by foes
The Army, through my help victorious rose
And stately *London*, (our great *Britain*'s glory)
My raging flame did make a mournful story,
But maugre all, that I, or foes could do
That *Phœnix* from her Bed, is risen New.
Old sacred *Zion*, I demolish'd thee.
So great *Diana*'s Temple was by me,   120
And more than bruitish *Sodom*, for her lust
With neighbouring Towns, I did consume to dust
What shall I say of Lightning and of Thunder
Which Kings and mighty ones amaze with wonder,
Which made a *Cæsar*, (*Romes*) the worlds proud head,
Foolish *Caligula* creep under's bed.
Of *Meteors*, *ignis fatuus* and the rest,
But to leave those to th'wise, I judge it best.
The rich I oft make poor, the strong I maime,
Not sparing Life when I can take the same;   130
And in a word, the world I shall consume
And all therein, at that great day of Doom;
Not before then, shall cease, my raging ire
And then because no matter more for fire:
Now Sisters pray proceed, each in your Course
As I, impart your usefulness and force.

Earth

The next in place Earth judg'd to be her due,
Sister (quoth shee) I come not short of you,
In wealth and use I do surpass you all,
And mother earth of old men did me call: 140
Such is my fruitfulness, an Epithite,
Which none ere gave, or you could claim of right
Among my praises this I count not least,
I am th'original of man and beast.

To tell what sundry fruits my fat soil yields
In Vineyards, Gardens, Orchards and Corn-fields,
Their kinds, their tasts, their colors and their smells
Would so pass time I could say nothing else:
The rich the poor, wise, fool, and every sort
Of these so common things can make report.　　150
To tell you of my countryes and my Regions,
Soon would they pass not hundreds but legions:
My cities famous, rich and populous,
Whose numbers now are grown innumerous.
I have not time to think of every part,
Yet let me name my *Grecia*, 'tis my heart.
For learning arms and arts I love it well,
But chiefly 'cause the *Muses* there did dwell.
Ile here skip ore my mountains reaching skyes,
Whether *Pyrenean*, or the *Alpes*, both lyes　　160
On either side the country of the *Gaules*
Strong forts, from *Spanish* and *Italian* brawles.
And huge great *Taurus* longer than the rest,
Dividing great *Armenia* from the least;
And *Hemus* whose steep sides none foot upon,
But farewell all for dear mount *Helicon*.
And wondrous high *Olimpus*, of such fame,
That heav'n it self was oft call'd by that name.
Parnassus sweet, I dote too much on thee,
Unless thou prove a better friend to me:　　170
But Ile leap ore these hills, not touch a dale,
Nor will I stay, no not in *Tempe* Vale,
Ile here let go my Lions of *Numedia*,
My Panthers and my Leopards of *Libia*,
The Behemoth and rare found Unicorn,
Poysons sure antidote lyes in his horn,
And my *Hiæna* (imitates mans voice)
Out of great numbers I might pick my choice,

Thousands in woods and plains, both wild and tame,
But here or there, I list now none to name: 180
No, though the fawning Dog did urge me sore,
In his behalf to speak a word the more,
Whose trust and valour I might here commend;
But time's too short and precious so to spend.
But hark you wealthy merchants, who for prize
Send forth your well-man'd ships where sun doth rise,
After three years when men and meat is spent,
My rich Commodityes pay double rent.
Ye *Galenists*, my Drugs that come from thence,
Do cure your Patients, fill your purse with pence;   190
Besides the use of roots, of hearbs and plants,
That with less cost near home supply your wants.
But Mariners where got you ships and Sails,
And Oars to row, when both my Sisters fails
Your Tackling, Anchor, compass too is mine,
Which guids when sun nor moon nor stars do shine
Ye mighty Kings, who for your lasting fames
Built Cities, Monuments, call'd by your names,
Were those compiled heaps of massy stones
That your ambition laid, ought but my bones?   200
Ye greedy misers, who do dig for gold
For gemms, for silver, Treasures which I hold,
Will not my goodly face your rage suffice
But you will see, what in my bowels lyes?
And ye Artificers, all Trades and sorts
My bounty calls you forth to make reports,
If ought you have, to use, to wear, to eat,
But what I freely yield, upon your sweat?
And Cholerick Sister, thou for all thine ire
Well knowst my fuel, must maintain thy fire.   210
As I ingenuously with thanks confess,
My cold thy fruitfull heat doth crave no less:

But how my cold dry temper works upon
The melancholy Constitution;
How the autumnal season I do sway,
And how I force the grey-head to obey,
I should here make a short, yet true Narration,
But that thy method is mine imitation.
Now must I shew mine adverse quality,
And how I oft work mans mortality: 220
He sometimes finds, maugre his toiling pain
Thistles and thorns where he expected grain.
My sap to plants and trees I must not grant,
The vine, the olive, and the figtree want:
The Corn and Hay do fall before the're mown,
And buds from fruitfull trees as soon as blown;
Then dearth prevails, that nature to suffice
The Mother on her tender infant flyes;
The husband knows no wife, nor father sons,
But to all outrages their hunger runs: 230
Dreadfull examples soon I might produce,
But to such Auditors 'twere of no use.
Again when Delvers dare in hope of gold
To ope those veins of *Mine*, audacious bold:
While they thus in mine entrails love to dive,
Before they know, they are inter'd alive.
Y'affrighted wights appal'd, how do ye shake,
When once you feel me your foundation quake?
Because in the Abbysse of my dark womb
Your cities and your selves I oft intomb: 240
O dreadfull Sepulcher! that this is true
Dathan and all his company well knew,
So did that Roman, far more stout than wise,
Bur'ing himself alive for honours prize.
And since fair *Italy* full sadly knowes
What she hath lost by these remed'less woes.

Again what veins of poyson in me lye,
Some kill outright, and some do stupifye:
Nay into herbs and plants it sometimes creeps,
In heats and colds and gripes and drowzy sleeps: 250
Thus I occasion death to man and beast
When food they seek, and harm mistrust the least.
Much might I say of the hot *Libian* sand
Which rise like tumbling Billows on the Land
Wherein *Cambyses* Armie was o'rethrown
(but windy Sister, 'twas when you have blown)
I'le say no more, but this thing add I must
Remember Sons, your mould is of my dust
And after death whether interr'd or burn'd
As Earth at first so into Earth return'd.   260

Water

Scarce Earth had done, but th'angry water mov'd
Sister (quoth she) it had full well behov'd
Among your boastings to have praised me
Cause of your fruitfulness as you shall see:
This your neglect shews your ingratitude
And how your subtilty, would men delude
Not one of us (all knows) that's like to thee
Ever in craving, from the other three;
But thou art bound to me, above the rest
Who am thy drink, thy blood, thy sap and best: 270
If I withhold what art thou? dead dry lump
Thou bearst nor grass or plant nor tree, nor stump
Thy extream thirst is moistned by my love
With springs below, and showres from above
Or else thy Sun-burnt face, and gaping chops
Complain to th' heavens, if I withhold my drops
Thy Bear, thy Tyger, and thy Lion stout,
When I am gone, their fiercenes none needs doubt

Thy Camel hath no strength, thy Bull no force
Nor mettal's found, in the couragious Horse   280
Hinds leave their calves, the Elephant the Fens
The wolves and savage beasts, forsake their Dens
The lofty Eagle, and the Stork fly low,
The Peacock and the Ostrich, share in woe,
The Pine, the Cedar, yea, and *Daphne*'s Tree
Do cease to flourish in this misery,
Man wants his bread and wine, and pleasant fruits
He knows, such sweets, lies not in Earths dry roots
Then seeks me out, in river and in well
His deadly malady I might expell: 290
If I supply, his heart and veins rejoyce,
If not, soon ends his life, as did his voyce;
That this is true, Earth thou canst not deny
I call thine *Egypt*, this to verifie,
Which by my fatting *Nile*, doth yield such store
That she can spare, when nations round are poor
When I run low, and not o'reflow her brinks
To meet with want, each woful man be-thinks:
And such I am, in Rivers, showrs and springs
But what's the wealth, that my rich Ocean brings   300
Fishes so numberless, I there do hold
If thou shouldst buy, it would exhaust thy gold:
There lives the oyly Whale, whom all men know
Such wealth but not such like, Earth thou maist show
The Dolphin loving musick, *Arians* friend
The witty Barbel, whose craft doth her commend
With thousands more, which now I list not name
Thy silence of thy Beasts doth cause the same
My pearles that dangle at thy Darlings ears,
Not thou, but shel-fish yield, as *Pliny* clears.   310
Was ever gem so rich found in thy trunk,
As *Egypts* wanton, *Cleopatra* drunk?

Or hast thou any colour can come nigh
The Roman purple, double *Tirian* Dye?
Which *Cæsars* Consuls, Tribunes all adorn,
For it to search my waves they thought no scorn.
Thy gallant rich perfuming Amber-greece
I lightly cast ashore as frothy fleece:
With rowling grains of purest massie gold,
Which *Spains Americans* do gladly hold.   320
Earth thou hast not moe countrys vales and mounds
Than I have fountains, rivers lakes and ponds.
My sundry seas, black, white and *Adriatique*,
Ionian, *Baltique* and the vast *Atlantique*,
Ægean, *Caspian*, golden Rivers five,
Asphaltis lake where nought remains alive:
But I should go beyond thee in my boasts,
If I should name more seas than thou hast Coasts.
And be thy mountains n'er so high and steep,
I soon can match them with my seas as deep.   330
To speak of kinds of waters I neglect,
My diverse fountains and their strange effect:
My wholsome bathes, together with their cures;
My water Syrens with their guilefull lures.
Th'uncertain cause of certain ebbs and flows,
Which wondring *Aristotles* wit n'er knows.
Nor will I speak of waters made by art,
Which can to life restore a fainting heart.
Nor fruitfull dews, nor drops distil'd from eyes,
Which pitty move, and oft deceive the wise: 340
Nor yet of salt and sugar, sweet and smart,
Both when we list to water we convert.
Alas thy ships and oars could do no good
Did they but want my Ocean and my flood.
The wary merchant on his weary beast
Transfers his goods from south to north and east,

Unless I ease his toil, and do transport
The wealthy fraight unto his wished port.
These be my benefits, which may suffice:
I now must shew what ill there in me lies.   350
The flegmy Constitution I uphold,
All humors, tumors which are bred of cold:
O're childhood and ore winter I bear sway,
And *Luna* for my Regent I obey.
As I with showers oft times refresh the earth,
So oft in my excess I cause a dearth,
And with abundant wet so cool the ground,
By adding cold to cold no fruit proves sound.
The Farmer and the Grasier do complain
Of rotten sheep, lean kine, and mildew'd grain.   360
And with my wasting floods and roaring torrent,
Their cattel hay and corn I sweep down current.
Nay many times my Ocean breaks his bounds,
And with astonishment the world confounds,
And swallows Countryes up, n'er seen again,
And that an island makes which once was Main:
Thus *Britain* fair (tis thought) was cut from *France*
Scicily from *Italy* by the like chance,
And but one land was *Africa* and *Spain*
Untill proud *Gibraltar* did make them twain.   370
Some say I swallow'd up (sure tis a notion)
A mighty country in th' *Atlantique Ocean*.
I need not say much of my hail and snow,
My ice and extream cold, which all men know,
Whereof the first so ominous I rain'd,
That *Israels* enemies therewith were brain'd:
And of my chilling snows such plenty be,
That *Caucasus* high mounts are seldome free.
Mine ice doth glaze *Europes* great rivers o're,
Till sun release, their ships can sail no more.   380

All know that inundations I have made,
Wherein not men, but mountains seem'd to wade;
As when *Achaia*, all under water stood,
That for two hundred years it n'er prov'd good.
Deucalions great Deluge with many moe,
But these are trifles to the flood of *Noe*,
Then wholly perish'd Earths ignoble race,
And to this day impairs her beauteous face,
That after times shall never feel like woe,
Her confirm'd sons behold my colour'd bow.   390
Much might I say of wracks, but that Ile spare,
And now give place unto our Sister *Air*.

Air

Content (quoth Air) to speak the last of you,
Yet am not ignorant first was my due:
I do suppose you'l yield without controul
I am the breath of every living soul.
Mortals, what one of you that loves not me
Abundantly more than my Sisters three?
And though you love Fire, Earth and Water well
Yet Air beyond all these you know t'excell.   400
I ask the man condemn'd, that's neer his death,
How gladly should his gold purchase his breath,
And all the wealth that ever earth did give,
How freely should it go so he might live:
No earth, thy witching trash were all but vain,
If my pure air thy sons did not sustain.
The famish'd thirsty man that craves supply,
His moving reason is, give least I dye,
So loth he is to go though nature's spent
To bid adieu to his dear Element.   410
Nay what are words which do reveal the mind,
Speak who or what they will they are but wind.

Your drums your trumpets and your organs sound,
What is't but forced air which doth rebound,
And such are ecchoes and report ofth' gun
That tells afar th'exploit which it hath done.
Your Songs and pleasant tunes they are the same,
And so's the notes which Nightingales do frame.
Ye forging Smiths, if bellows once were gone
Your red hot work more coldly would go on.   420
Ye Mariners, tis I that fill your sails,
And speed you to your port with wished gales.
When burning heat doth cause you faint, I cool,
And when I smile, your ocean's like a pool.
I help to ripe the corn, I turn the mill,
And with my self I every *Vacuum* fill.
The ruddy sweet sanguine is like to air,
And youth and spring, Sages to me compare,
My moist hot nature is so purely thin,
No place so subtilly made, but I get in.   430
I grow more pure and pure as I mount higher,
And when I'm throughly rarifi'd turn fire:
So when I am condens'd, I turn to water,
Which may be done by holding down my vapour.
Thus I another body can assume,
And in a trice my own nature resume.
Some for this cause of late have been so bold
Me for no Element longer to hold,
Let such suspend their thoughts, and silent be,
For all Philosophers make one of me: 440
And what those Sages either spake or writ
Is more authentick than our modern wit.
Next of my fowles such multitudes there are,
Earths beasts and waters fish scarce can compare.
Th'Ostrich with her plumes, th'Eagle with her eyn
The Phænix too (if any be) are mine,

The stork, the crane, the partridg, and the phesant
The Thrush, the wren, the lark a prey to'th' pesant.
With thousands more which now I may omit
Without impeachment to my tale or wit.   450
As my fresh air preserves all things in life,
So when corrupt, mortality is rife:
Then Fevers, Purples, Pox and Pestilence,
With divers moe, work deadly consequence:
Whereof such multitudes have di'd and fled,
The living scarce had power to bury dead;
Yea so contagious countryes have we known
That birds have not 'scapt death as they have flown,
Of murrain, cattle numberless did fall,
Men fear'd destruction epidemical.   460
Then of my tempests felt at sea and land,
Which neither ships nor houses could withstand,
What wofull wracks I've made may well appear,
If nought were known but that before *Algere*,
Where famous *Charles the fifth* more loss sustaind
Than in his long hot war which *Millain* gain'd.
Again what furious storms and Hurricanoes
Know western Isles, as *Christophers*, *Barbadoes*,
Where neither houses, trees nor plants I spare;
But some fall down, and some fly up with air.   470
Earthquakes so hurtfull, and so fear'd of all,
Imprison'd I, am the original.
Then what prodigious sights I sometimes show,
As battles pitcht in th' air, as countryes know,
Their joyning fighting, forcing and retreat,
That earth appears in heaven, O wonder great!
Sometimes red flaming swords and blazing stars,
Portentous signs of famines, plagues and wars.
Which make the mighty Monarchs fear their fates
By death or great mutation of their States.   480

I have said less than did my Sisters three,
But what's their worth or force, the same's in me.
To adde to all I've said was my intent,
But dare not go beyond my Element.

Of the four Humours in Mans Constitution

The former four now ending their discourse,
Ceasing to vaunt their good, or threat their force,
Lo other four step up, crave leave to show
The native qualityes that from them flow:
But first they wisely shew'd their high descent,
Each eldest daughter to each Element.
Choler was own'd by fire, and Blood by air,
Earth knew her black swarth child, water her fair:
All having made obeysance to each Mother,
Had leave to speak, succeeding one the other: 10
But 'mongst themselves they were at variance,
Which of the four should have predominance.
Choler first hotly claim'd right by her mother,
Who had precedency of all the other:
But Sanguine did disdain what she requir'd,
Pleading her self was most of all desir'd.
Proud Melancholy more envious than the rest,
The second, third or last could not digest.
She was the silentest of all the four,
Her wisdom spake not much, but thought the more   20
Mild Flegme did not contest for chiefest place,
Only she crav'd to have a vacant space.
Well, thus they parle and chide; but to be brief,
Or will they, nill they, Choler will be chief.

They seing her impetuosity
At present yielded to necessity.

Choler

To shew my high descent and pedegree,
Your selves would judge but vain prolixity;
It is acknowledged from whence I came,
It shall suffice to shew you what I am,   30
My self and mother one, as you shall see,
But shee in greater, I in less degree.
We both once Masculines, the world doth know,
Now Feminines awhile, for love we owe
Unto your Sisterhood, which makes us render
Our noble selves in a less noble gender.
Though under Fire we comprehend all heat,
Yet man for Choler is the proper seat:
I in his heart erect my regal throne,
Where Monarch like I play and sway alone. 40
Yet many times unto my great disgrace
One of your selves are my Compeers in place,
Where if your rule prove once predominant,
The man proves boyish, sottish, ignorant:
But if you yield subservience unto me,
I make a man, a man in th'high'st degree:
Be he a souldier, I more fence his heart
Than iron Corslet 'gainst a sword or dart.
What makes him face his foe without appal,
To storm a breach, or scale a city wall, 50
In dangers to account himself more sure
Than timerous Hares whom Castles do immure?
Have you not heard of worthyes, Demi-Gods?
Twixt them and others what is't makes the odds
But valour? whence comes that? from none of you,
Nay milksops at such brunts you look but blew.

Here's sister ruddy, worth the other two,
Who much will talk, but little dares she do,
Unless to Court and claw, to dice and drink,
And there she will out-bid us all, I think,   60
She loves a fiddle better than a drum,
A Chamber well, in field she dares not come,
She'l ride a horse as bravely as the best,
And break a staff, provided 'be in jest;
But shuns to look on wounds, and blood that's spilt,
She loves her sword only because its gilt.
Then here's our sad black Sister, worse than you.
She'l neither say she will, nor will she doe;
But peevish Malecontent, musing she sits,
And by misprissions like to loose her witts: 70
If great perswasions cause her meet her foe,
In her dull resolution she's so slow,
To march her pace to some is greater pain
Than by a quick encounter to be slain.
But be she beaten, she'l not run away,
She'l first advise if't be not best to stay.
Now let's give cold white sister flegme her right,
So loving unto all she scorns to fight:
If any threaten her, she'l in a trice
Convert from water to congealed ice: 80
Her teeth will chatter, dead and wan's her face,
And 'fore she be assaulted, quits the place.
She dares not challeng, if I speak amiss,
Nor hath she wit or heat to blush at this.
Here's three of you all see now what you are,
Then yield to me preheminence in war.
Again who fits for learning, science, arts?
Who rarifies the intellectual parts:
From whence fine spirits flow and witty notions:
But tis not from our dull, slow sisters motions: 90

Nor sister sanguine, from thy moderate heat,
Poor spirits the Liver breeds, which is thy seat.
What comes from thence, my heat refines the same
And through the arteries sends it o're the frame:
The vital spirits they're call'd, and well they may
For when they fail, man turns unto his clay.
The animal I claim as well as these,
The nerves, should I not warm, soon would they freeze
But flegme her self is now provok'd at this
She thinks I never shot so far amiss.   100
The brain she challengeth, the head's her seat;
But know'ts a foolish brain that wanteth heat.
My absence proves it plain, her wit then flyes
Out at her nose, or melteth at her eyes.
Oh who would miss this influence of thine
To be distill'd, a drop on every Line?
Alas, thou hast no Spirits; thy Company
Will feed a dropsy, or a Tympany,
The Palsy, Gout, or Cramp, or some such dolour:
Thou wast not made, for Souldier or for Scholar;   110
Of greazy paunch, and bloated cheeks go vaunt,
But a good head from these are dissonant.
But Melancholy, wouldst have this glory thine,
Thou sayst thy wits are staid, subtil and fine;
'Tis true, when I am Midwife to thy birth
Thy self's as dull, as is thy mother Earth:
Thou canst not claim the liver, head nor heart
Yet hast thy Seat assign'd, a goodly part
The sinke of all us three, the hateful Spleen
Of that black Region, nature made thee Queen;   120
Where pain and sore obstruction thou dost work,
Where envy, malice, thy Companions lurk.
If once thou'rt great, what follows thereupon

But bodies wasting, and destruction?
So base thou art, that baser cannot be,
Th' excrement adustion of me.
But I am weary to dilate your shame,
Nor is't my pleasure thus to blur your name,
Only to raise my honour to the Skies,
As objects best appear by contraries.   130
Both Arms, and Arts I claim, and higher things,
The princely qualities befitting Kings,
Whose profound heads I line with policies,
They'r held for Oracles, they are so wise,
Their wrathful looks are death their words are laws
Their Courage friend and foe and Subject awes;
But one of you, would make a worthy King
Like our sixth *Henry* (that same virtuous thing)
That when a Varlet struck him o're the side,
Forsooth you are to blame, he grave reply'd.   140
Take Choler from a Prince, what is he more
Than a dead Lion, by Beasts triumph'd o're.
Again you know, how I act every part
But th' influence, I still send from the heart:
It's nor your Muscles, nerves, nor this nor that
Do's ought without my lively heat, that's flat:
Nay th' stomack magazine to all the rest
Without my boyling heat cannot digest:
And yet to make my greatness, still more great
What differences, the Sex? but only heat.   150
And one thing more, to close up my narration
Of all that lives, I cause the propagation.
I have been sparing what I might have said
I love no boasting, that's but Childrens trade.
To what you now shall say I will attend,
And to your weakness gently condescend.

Good Sisters, give me leave, as is my place
To vent my grief, and wipe off my disgrace:
Your selves may plead your wrongs are no whit less
Your patience more than mine, I must confess   160
Did ever sober tongue such language speak,
Or honesty such tyes unfriendly break?
Dost know thy self so well us so amiss?
Is't arrogance or folly causeth this?
Ile only shew the wrong thou'st done to me,
Then let my sisters right their injury.
To pay with railings is not mine intent,
But to evince the truth by Argument:
I will analyze this thy proud relation
So full of boasting and prevarication,   170
Thy foolish incongruityes Ile show,
So walk thee till thou'rt cold, then let thee go.
There is no Souldier but thy self (thou sayest,)
No valour upon Earth, but what thou hast
Thy silly provocations I despise,
And leave't to all to judge, where valour lies.
No pattern, nor no pattron will I bring
But *David*, *Judah*'s most heroick King,
Whose glorious deeds in Arms the world can tell,
A rosie cheek Musitian thou know'st well;   180
He knew well how to handle Sword and Harp,
And how to strike full sweet, as well as sharp,
Thou laugh'st at me for loving merriment,
And scorn'st all Knightly sports at Turnament.
Thou sayst I love my Sword, because it's gilt,
But know, I love the Blade, more than the Hilt,
Yet do abhor such temerarious deeds,
As thy unbridled, barbarous Choler breeds:

Thy rudeness counts good manners vanity,
And real Complements base flattery.   190
For drink, which of us twain like it the best,
Ile go no further than thy nose for test:
Thy other scoffs, not worthy of reply
Shall vanish as of no validity:
Of thy black Calumnies this is but part,
But now Ile shew what souldier thou art.
And though thou'st us'd me with opprobrious spight
My ingenuity must give thee right.
Thy choler is but rage when tis most pure,
But usefull when a mixture can endure;   200
As with thy mother fire, so tis with thee,
The best of all the four when they agree:
But let her leave the rest, then I presume
Both them and all things else she would consume.
Whilst us for thine associates thou tak'st,
A Souldier most compleat in all points mak'st:
But when thou scorn'st to take the help we lend,
Thou art a Fury or infernal Fiend.
Witness the execrable deeds thou'st done,
Nor sparing Sex nor Age, nor Sire nor Son;   210
To satisfie thy pride and cruelty,
Thou oft hast broke bounds of Humanity.
Nay should I tell, thou would'st count me no blab,
How often for the lye, thou'st given the stab.
To take the wall's a sin of so high rate,
That nought but death the same may expiate,
To cross thy will, a challenge doth deserve
So shed'st that blood, thou'rt bounden to preserve
Wilt thou this valour, Courage, Manhood call:
No, know 'tis pride most diabolical.   220
If murthers be thy glory, tis no less,
Ile not envy thy feats, nor happiness:

But if in fitting time and place 'gainst foes
For countreys good thy life thou dar'st expose,
Be dangers n'er so high, and courage great,
Ile praise that prowess, fury, Choler, heat:
But such thou never art when all alone,
Yet such when we all four are joyn'd in one.
And when such thou art, even such are we,
The friendly Coadjutors still of thee.   230
Nextly the Spirits thou dost wholly claim,
Which nat'ral, vital, animal we name:
To play Philosopher I have no list,
Nor yet Physitian, nor Anatomist,
For acting these, I have no will nor Art,
Yet shall with Equity, give thee thy part
For natural, thou dost not much contest;
For there is none (thou sayst) if some not best;
That there are some, and best, I dare averre
Of greatest use, if reason do not erre: 240
What is there living, which do'nt first derive
His Life now Animal, from vegetive:
If thou giv'st life, I give the nourishment,
Thine without mine, is not, 'tis evident:
But I without thy help, can give a growth
As plants trees, and small Embryon know'th
And if vital Spirits, do flow from thee
I am as sure, the natural, from me:
Be thine the nobler, which I grant, yet mine
Shall justly claim priority of thine.   250
I am the fountain which thy Cistern fills
Through warm blew Conduits of my venial rills:
What hath the heart, but what's sent from the liver
If thou'rt the taker, I must be the giver.
Then never boast of what thou dost receive:
For of such glory I shall thee bereave.

But why the heart should be usurp'd by thee,
I must confess seems something strange to me:
The spirits through thy heat made perfect are,
But the Materials none of thine, that's clear: 260
Their wondrous mixture is of blood and air,
The first my self, second my mother fair.
But Ile not force retorts, nor do thee wrong,
Thy fi'ry yellow froth is mixt among,
Challeng not all, 'cause part we do allow;
Thou know'st I've there to do as well as thou:
But thou wilt say I deal unequally,
There lives the irascible faculty,
Which without all dispute, is Cholers own;
Besides the vehement heat, only there known   270
Can be imputed, unto none but Fire
Which is thy self, thy Mother and thy Sire
That this is true, I easily can assent
If still you take along my Aliment;
And let me be your partner which is due,
So shall I give the dignity to you:
Again, Stomacks Concoction thou dost claim,
But by what right, nor do'st, nor canst thou name
Unless as heat, it be thy faculty,
And so thou challengest her property.   280
The help she needs, the loving liver lends,
Who th' benefit o'th' whole ever intends:
To meddle further I shall be but shent,
Th'rest to our Sisters is more pertinent;
Your slanders thus refuted takes no place,
Nor what you've said, doth argue my disgrace,
Now through your leaves, some little time I'l spend
My worth in humble manner to commend
This, hot, moist nutritive humour of mine
When 'tis untaint, pure, and most genuine   290

Shall chiefly take the place, as is my due
Without the least indignity to you.
Of all your qualities I do partake,
And what you single are, the whole I make
Your hot, moist, cold, dry natures are but four,
I moderately am all, what need I more;
As thus, if hot then dry, if moist, then cold,
If this you cann't disprove, then all I hold
My virtues hid, I've let you dimly see
My sweet Complection proves the verity.   300
This Scarlet die's a badge of what's within
One touch thereof, so beautifies the skin:
Nay, could I be, from all your tangs but pure
Mans life to boundless Time might still endure.
But here one thrusts her heat, wher'ts not requir'd
So suddenly, the body all is fired,
And of the calme sweet temper quite bereft,
Which makes the Mansion, by the Soul soon left.
So Melancholy seizes on a man,
With her unchearful visage, swarth and wan,   310
The body dryes, the mind sublime doth smother,
And turns him to the womb of's earthy mother:
And flegm likewise can shew her cruel art,
With cold distempers to pain every part:
The lungs she rots, the body wears away,
As if she'd leave no flesh to turn to clay,
Her languishing diseases, though not quick
At length demolishes the Faberick,
All to prevent, this curious care I take,
In th' last concoction segregation make   320
Of all the perverse humours from mine own,
The bitter choler most malignant known
I turn into his Cell close by my side
The Melancholy to the Spleen t'abide:

Likewise the whey, some use I in the veins,
The overplus I send unto the reins:
But yet for all my toil, my care and skill,
Its doom'd by an irrevocable will
That my intents should meet with interruption,
That mortal man might turn to his corruption.   330
I might here shew the nobleness of mind
Of such as to the sanguine are inclin'd,
They're liberal, pleasant, kind and courteous,
And like the Liver all benignious.
For arts and sciences they are the fittest;
And maugre Choler still they are the wittiest:
With an ingenious working Phantasie,
A most voluminous large Memory,
And nothing wanting but Solidity.
But why alas, thus tedious should I be,   340
Thousand examples you may daily see.
If time I have transgrest, and been too long,
Yet could not be more brief without much wrong;
I've scarce wip'd off the spots proud choler cast,
Such venome lies in words, though but a blast:
No braggs I've us'd, to you I dare appeal,
If modesty my worth do not conceal.
I've us'd no bitternesse nor taxt your name,
As I to you, to me do ye the same.

Melancholy

He that with two Assailants hath to do,   350
Had need be armed well and active too.
Especially when friendship is pretended,
The blow's most deadly where it is intended.
Though choler rage and rail, I'le not do so,
The tongue's no weapon to assault a foe:

But sith we fight with words, we might be kind
To spare our selves and beat the whistling wind,
Fair rosie sister, so might'st thou scape free;
I'le flatter for a time as thou didst me:
But when the first offender I have laid,   360
Thy soothing girds shall fully be repaid.
But Choler be thou cool'd or chaf'd, I'le venter,
And in contentions lists now justly enter.
What mov'd thee thus to vilifie my name,
Not past all reason, but in truth all shame:
Thy fiery spirit shall bear away this prize,
To play such furious pranks I am too wise:
If in a Souldier rashness be so precious,
Know in a General tis most pernicious.
Nature doth teach to shield the head from harm,   370
The blow that's aim'd thereat is latcht by th'arm.
When in Batalia my foes I face
I then command proud Choler stand thy place,
To use thy sword, thy courage and thy art
There to defend my self, thy better part.
This wariness count not for cowardize,
He is not truly valiant that's not wise.
It's no less glory to defend a town,
Than by assault to gain one not our own;
And if *Marcellus* bold be call'd *Romes* sword,   380
Wise *Fabius* is her buckler all accord:
And if thy hast my slowness should not temper,
'Twere but a mad irregular distemper;
Enough of that by our sisters heretofore,
Ile come to that which wounds me somewhat more:
Of learning, policy thou wouldst bereave me,
But 's not thine ignorance shall thus deceive me:
What greater Clark or Politician lives,
Than he whose brain a touch my humour gives?

What is too hot my coldness doth abate,   390
What's diffluent I do consolidate.
If I be partial judg'd or thought to erre,
The melancholy snake shall it aver,
Whose cold dry head more subtilty doth yield,
Than all the huge beasts of the fertile field.
Again thou dost confine me to the spleen,
As of that only part I were the Queen,
Let me as well make thy precincts the Gall,
So prison thee within that bladder small:
Reduce the man to's principles, then see   400
If I have not more part than all you three:
What is within, without, of theirs or thine,
Yet time and age shall soon declare it mine.
When death doth seize the man your stock is lost,
When you poor bankrupts prove then have I most.
You'l say here none shall e're disturb my right,
You high born from that lump then take your flight.
Then who's mans friend, when life and all forsakes?
His Mother mine, him to her womb retakes:
Thus he is ours, his portion is the grave,   410
But while he lives, I'le shew what part I have:
And first the firm dry bones I justly claim,
The strong foundation of the stately frame:
Likewise the usefull Spleen, though not the best,
Yet is a bowel call'd well as the rest:
The Liver, Stomack, owe their thanks of right,
The first it drains, of th'last quicks appetite.
Laughter (tho' thou say malice) flows from hence,
These two in one cannot have residence.
But thou most grosly dost mistake to think   420
The Spleen for all you three was made a sink,
Of all the rest thou'st nothing there to do,
But if thou hast, that malice is from you.

Again you often touch my swarthy hue,
That black is black, and I am black tis true;
But yet more comely far I dare avow,
Than is thy torrid nose or brazen brow.
But that which shews how high your spight is bent
Is charging me to be thy excrement:
Thy loathsome imputation I defie, 430
So plain a slander needeth no reply.
When by thy heat thou'st bak'd thy self to crust,
And so art call'd black Choler or adust,
Thou witless think'st that I am thy excretion,
So mean thou art in Art as in discretion:
But by your leave I'le let your greatness see
What Officer thou art to us all three,
The Kitchin Drudge, the cleanser of the sinks
That casts out all that man e're eats or drinks:
If any doubt the truth whence this should come, 440
Shew them thy passage to th' Duodenum;
Thy biting quality still irritates,
Till filth and thee nature exonerates:
If there thou'rt stopt, to th' Liver thou turn'st in,
And thence with jaundies saffrons all the skin.
No further time Ile spend in confutation,
I trust I've clear'd your slanderous imputation.
I now speak unto all, no more to one,
Pray hear, admire and learn instruction.
My virtues yours surpass without compare, 450
The first my constancy that jewel rare:
Choler's too rash this golden gift to hold,
And Sanguine is more fickle manifold,
Here, there her restless thoughts do ever fly,
Constant in nothing but unconstancy.
And what Flegme is, we know, like to her mother,
Unstable is the one, and so the other;

With me is noble patience also found,
Impatient Choler loveth not the sound,
What sanguine is, she doth not heed nor care,   460
Now up, now down, transported like the Air:
Flegme's patient because her nature's tame;
But I, by virtue do acquire the same.
My Temperance, Chastity is eminent,
But these with you, are seldome resident;
Now could I stain my ruddy Sisters face
With deeper red, to shew you her disgrace,
But rather I with silence vaile her shame
Than cause her blush, while I relate the same.
Nor are ye free from this inormity,   470
Although she bear the greatest obloquie,
My prudence, judgement, I might now reveal
But wisdom 'tis my wisdome to conceal.
Unto diseases not inclin'd as you,
Nor cold, nor hot, Ague nor Plurisie,
Nor Cough, nor Quinsey, nor the burning Feaver,
I rarely feel to act his fierce endeavour;
My sickness in conceit chiefly doth lye,
What I imagine that's my malady.
Chymeraes strange are in my phantasy,   480
And things that never were, nor shall I see.
I love not talk. Reason lies not in length,
Nor multitude of words argues our strength;
I've done pray sister Flegme proceed in Course,
We shall expect much sound, but little force.

Flegme

Patient I am, patient I'd need to be,
To bear with the injurious taunts of three,
Though wit I want, and anger I have less,
Enough of both, my wrongs now to express

I've not forgot, how bitter Choler spake   490
Nor how her gaul on me she causeless brake;
Nor wonder 'twas for hatred there's not small,
Where opposition is Diametrical.
To what is Truth I freely will assent,
Although my Name do suffer detriment,
What's slanderous repell, doubtful dispute,
And when I've nothing left to say be mute.
Valour I want, no Souldier am 'tis true,
I'le leave that manly Property to you;
I love no thundring guns, nor bloody wars,   500
My polish'd Skin was not ordain'd for Skarrs:
But though the pitched field I've ever fled,
At home the Conquerours have conquered.
Nay, I could tell you what's more true than meet,
That Kings have laid their Scepters at my feet;
When Sister sanguine paints my Ivory face:
The Monarchs bend and sue, but for my grace;
My lilly white when joyned with her red,
Princes hath slav'd, and Captains captived,
Country with Country, Greece with *Asia* fights   510
Sixty nine Princes, all stout *Hero* Knights.
Under *Troys* walls ten years will wear away,
Rather than loose one beauteous *Helena*.
But 'twere as vain, to prove this truth of mine
As at noon day, to tell the Sun doth shine.
Next difference that 'twixt us twain doth lye
Who doth possess the brain, or thou or I?
Shame forc'd thee say, the matter that was mine,
But the Spirits by which it acts are thine:
Thou speakest Truth, and I can say no less,   520
Thy heat doth much, I candidly confess;
Yet without ostentation I may say,
I do as much for thee another way:

And though I grant, thou art my helper here,
No debtor I because it's paid else where.
With all your flourishes, now Sisters three
Who is't that dare, or can, compare with me,
My excellencies are so great, so many,
I am confounded; fore I speak of any:
The brain's the noblest member all allow,   530
Its form and Scituation will avow,
Its Ventricles, Membranes and wondrous net,
Galen, *Hippocrates* drive to a set;
That Divine Ofspring the immortal Soul
Though it in all, and every part be whole,
Within this stately place of eminence,
Doth doubtless keep its mighty residence.
And surely, the Soul sensitive here lives,
Which life and motion to each creature gives,
The Conjugation of the parts, to th' braine   540
Doth shew, hence flow the pow'rs which they retain
Within this high Built *Cittadel*, doth lye
The Reason, fancy, and the memory;
The faculty of speech doth here abide,
The Spirits animal, from hence do slide:
The five most noble Senses here do dwell;
Of three it's hard to say, which doth excell.
This point now to discuss, 'longs not to me,
I'le touch the sight, great'st wonder of the three;
The optick Nerve, Coats, humours all are mine,   550
The watry, glassie, and the Chrystaline;
O mixture strange! O colour colourless,
Thy perfect temperament who can express:
He was no fool who thought the soul lay there,
Whence her affections passions speak so clear.
O good, O bad, O true, O traiterous eyes
What wonderments within your Balls there lyes,

Of all the Senses sight shall be the Queen;
Yet some may wish, O had mine eyes ne're seen.
Mine, likewise is the marrow, of the back,   560
Which runs through all the Spondles of the rack,
It is the substitute o'th royal brain,
All Nerves, except seven pair, to it retain.
And the strong Ligaments from hence arise,
Which joynt to joynt, the intire body tyes.
Some other parts there issue from the Brain,
Whose worth and use to tell, I must refrain:
Some curious learned *Crooke*, may these reveal
But modesty, hath charg'd me to conceal
Here's my Epitome of excellence: 570
For what's the Brains is mine by Consequence.
A foolish brain (quoth Choler) wanting heat
But a mad one say I, where 'tis too great,
Phrenzie's worse than folly, one would more glad
With a tame fool converse than with a mad;
For learning then my brain is not the fittest,
Nor will I yield that Choler is the wittiest.
Thy judgement is unsafe, thy fancy little,
For memory the sand is not more brittle;
Again, none's fit for Kingly state but thou,   580
If Tyrants be the best, I'le it allow:
But if love be as requisite as fear,
Then thou and I must make a mixture here.
Well to be brief, I hope now Cholers laid,
And I'le pass by what Sister sanguine said.
To Melancholy I'le make no reply,
The worst she said was instability,
And too much talk, both which I here confess
A warning good, hereafter I'le say less.
Let's now be friends; its time our spight were spent,   590
Lest we too late this rashness do repent,

Such premises will force a sad conclusion,
Unless we agree, all falls into confusion.
Let Sangine with her hot hand Choler hold,
To take her moist my moisture will be bold:
My cold, cold melancholy hand shall clasp;
Her dry, dry Cholers other hand shall grasp.
Two hot, two moist, two cold, two dry here be,
A golden Ring, the Posey *Unity*.
Nor jarrs nor scoffs, let none hereafter see,   600
But all admire our perfect Amity
Nor be discern'd, here's water, earth, air, fire,
But here's a compact body, whole intire.
This loving counsel pleas'd them all so well
That Flegme was judg'd for kindness to excell.

Of the four Ages of Man

Lo now four other act upon the stage,
Childhood and Youth, the Manly and Old age;
The first son unto flegm, Grand-child to water,
Unstable, supple, cold and moist's his nature.
The second frolick, claims his pedegree
From blood and air, for hot and moist is he.
The third of fire and Choler is compos'd
Vindicative and quarrelsome dispos'd.
The last of earth, and heavy melancholy,
Solid, hating all lightness and all folly.   10
Childhood was cloth'd in white and green to show
His spring was intermixed with some snow:
Upon his head nature a Garland set
Of Primrose, Daizy and the Violet.

Such cold mean flowrs the spring puts forth betime
Before the sun hath throughly heat the clime.
His Hobby striding did not ride but run,
And in his hand an hour-glass new begun,
In danger every moment of a fall,
And when tis broke then ends his life and all: 20
But if he hold till it have run its last,
Then may he live out threescore years or past.
Next Youth came up in gorgeous attire,
(As that fond age doth most of all desire)
His Suit of Crimson and his scarfe of green,
His pride in's countenance was quickly seen,
Garland of roses, pinks and gilli-flowers
Seemed on's head to grow bedew'd with showers:
His face as fresh as is *Aurora* fair,
When blushing she first 'gins to light the air.   30
No wooden horse, but one of mettal try'd,
He seems to fly or swim, and not to ride.
Then prancing on the stage, about he wheels,
But as he went death waited at his heels.
The next came up in a much graver sort,
As one that cared for a good report,
His sword by's side, and choler in his eyes,
But neither us'd as yet, for he was wise:
Of Autumns fruits a basket on his arm,
His golden God in's purse, which was his charm.   40
And last of all to act upon this stage
Leaning upon his staff came up Old Age,
Under his arm a sheaf of wheat he bore,
An harvest of the best, what needs he more?
In's other hand a glass ev'n almost run,
Thus writ about *This out then am I done.*
His hoary hairs, and grave aspect made way,
And all gave ear to what he had to say.

These being met each in his equipage
Intend to speak according to their age: 50
But wise Old age did with all gravity
To childish Childhood give precedency,
And to the rest his reason mildly told,
That he was young before he grew so old.
To do as he each one full soon assents,
Their method was that of the Elements,
That each should tell what of himself he knew,
Both good and bad, but yet no more than's true.
With heed now stood three ages of frail man,
To hear the child, who crying thus began: 60

Childhood

Ah me! conceiv'd in sin and born with sorrow,
A nothing, here to day and gone to morrow,
Whose mean beginning blushing can't reveal,
But night and darkness must with shame conceal.
My mothers breeding sickness I will spare,
Her nine moneths weary burthen not declare.
To shew her bearing pains, I should do wrong,
To tell those pangs which can't be told by tongue:
With tears into the world I did arrive,
My mother still did waste as I did thrive,   70
Who yet with love and all alacrity,
Spending, was willing to be spent for me.
With wayward cryes I did disturb her rest,
Who sought still to appease me with the breast:
With weary arms she danc'd and *By By* sung,
When wretched I ingrate had done the wrong.
When infancy was past, my childishness
Did act all folly that it could express,
My silliness did only take delight
In that which riper age did scorn and slight.   80

In Rattles, Baubles and such toyish stuff,
My then ambitious thoughts were low enough:
My high-born soul so straightly was confin'd,
That its own worth it did not know nor mind:
This little house of flesh did spacious count,
Through ignorance all troubles did surmount;
Yet this advantage had mine ignorance
Freedom from envy and from arrogance.
How to be rich or great I did not cark,
A Baron or a Duke ne'r made my mark,   90
Nor studious was Kings favours how to buy,
With costly presence or base flattery:
No office coveted wherein I might
Make strong my self and turn aside weak right:
No malice bare to this or that great Peer,
Nor unto buzzing whisperers gave ear:
I gave no hand nor vote for death or life,
I'd nought to do 'twixt King and peoples strife.
No Statist I, nor Martilist in'th field,
Where ere I went mine innocence was shield.   100
My quarrels not for Diadems did rise,
But for an apple, plum, or some such prize:
My strokes did cause no blood no wounds or skars,
My little wrath did end soon as my Warrs:
My Duel was no challeng nor did seek
My foe should weltring in his bowels reek.
I had no suits at law neighbours to vex,
Nor evidence for lands did me perplex.
I fear'd no storms, nor all the wind that blowes,
I had no ships at sea; nor fraights to loose.   110
I fear'd no drought nor wet, I had no crop,
Nor yet on future things did set my hope.
This was mine innocence, but ah! the seeds
Lay raked up of all the cursed weeds

Which sprouted forth in mine ensuing age,
As he can tel that next comes on the stage:
But yet let me relate before I go
The sins and dangers I am subject to,
Stained from birth with *Adams* sinfull fact,
Thence I began to sin as soon as act: 120
A perverse will, a love to what's forbid,
A serpents sting in pleasing face lay hid:
A lying tongue as soon as it could speak,
And fifth Commandment do daily break.
Oft stubborn, peevish, sullen, pout and cry,
Then nought can please, and yet I know not why.
As many are my sins, so dangers too;
For sin brings sorrow, sickness death and woe:
And though I miss the tossings of the mind,
Yet griefs in my frail flesh I still do find.   130
What gripes of wind mine infancy did pain,
What tortures I in breeding teeth sustain?
What crudityes my stomack cold hath bred,
Whence vomits, flux and worms have issued?
What breaches, knocks and falls I daily have,
And some perhaps I carry to my grave,
Sometimes in fire, sometimes in water fall,
Strangly preserv'd, yet mind it not at all:
At home, abroad my dangers manifold,
That wonder tis, my glass till now doth hold.   140
I've done; unto my elders I give way,
For tis but little that a child can say.

    Youth

My goodly cloathing, and my beauteous skin
Declare some greater riches are within:
But what is best I'le first present to view,
And then the worst in a more ugly hue:

For thus to doe we on this stage assemble,
Then let not him that hath most craft dissemble.
My education and my learning such,
As might my self and others profit much;   150
With nurture trained up in virtues schools
Of science, arts and tongues I know the rules,
The manners of the court I also know,
And so likewise what they in'th Country doe.
The brave attempts of valiant knights I prize,
That dare scale walls and forts rear'd to the skies.
The snorting Horse, the trumpet, Drum I like,
The glitt'ring sword, the Pistol and the Pike:
I cannot lye intrench'd before a town,
Nor wait till good success our hopes doth crown: 160
I scorn the heavy Corslet, musket-proof;
I fly to catch the bullet thats aloof.
Though thus in field, at home to all most kind,
So affable, that I can suit each mind.
I can insinuate into the breast,
And by my mirth can raise the heart deprest:
Sweet musick raps my brave harmonious soul,
My high thoughts elevate beyond the pole:
My wit, my bounty, and my courtesie,
Make all to place their future hopes on me.   170
This is my best, but Youth is known, Alas!
To be as wild as is the snuffing Ass:
As vain as froth, or vanity can be,
That who would see vain man, may look on me.
My gifts abusd, my education lost,
My wofull Parents longing hopes are crost,
My wit evaporates in merriment,
My valour in some beastly quarrell's spent:
My lust doth hurry me to all that's ill:
I know no law nor reason but my will.   180

Sometimes lay wait to take a wealthy purse,
Or stab the man in's own defence (that's worse)
Sometimes I cheat (unkind) a female heir
Of all at once, who not so wise as fair
Trusteth my loving looks and glozing tongue,
Untill her friends, treasure and honour's gone.
Sometimes I sit carousing others health,
Untill mine own be gone, my wit and wealth.
From pipe to pot, from pot to words and blows,
For he that loveth wine, wanteth no woes.   190
Whole nights with Ruffins, Roarers Fidlers spend,
To all obscenity mine ears I lend:
All Counsell hate, which tends to make me wise,
And dearest friends count for mine enemies.
If any care I take tis to be fine,
For sure my suit, more than my virtues shine
If time from leud Companions I can spare,
'Tis spent to curle, and pounce my new-bought hair.
Some new *Adonis* I do strive to be;
Sardanapalus now survives in me.   200
Cards, Dice, and Oathes concomitant I love,
To playes, to masques, to Taverns still I move.
And in a word, if what I am you'd hear,
Seek out a *Brittish* bruitish Cavaleer:
Such wretch, such Monster am I, but yet more,
I have no heart at all this to deplore,
Remembring not the dreadfull day of doom,
Nor yet that heavy reckoning soon to come.
Though dangers do attend me every hour,
And gastly Death oft threats me with his power,   210
Sometimes by wounds in idle Combates taken,
Sometimes with Agues all my body shaken:
Sometimes by fevers, all my moisture drinking,
My heart lies frying, and mine eyes are sinking,

Sometimes the Quinsey, painfull Pleurisie,
With sad affrights of death doth menace me:
Sometimes the two fold Pox me sore bemarrs
With outward marks, and inward loathsome scarrs,
Sometimes the Phrenzy strangly mads my brain,
That oft for it in *Bedlam* I remain.   220
Too many my diseases to recite,
That wonder tis, I yet behold the light,
That yet my bed in darkness is not made,
And I in black oblivions Den now laid.
Of aches full my bones, of woe my heart,
Clapt in that prison, never thence to start.
Thus I have said, and what I've been, you see
Childhood and Youth are vain yea vanity.

Middle Age

Childhood and Youth (forgot) I've sometimes seen
And now am grown more staid who have bin green   230
What they have done, the same was done by me,
As was their praise or shame, so mine must be.
Now age is more; more good you may expect,
But more mine age, the more is my defect.
When my wild oates were sown and ripe and mown
I then receiv'd an harvest of mine own.
My reason then bad judge how little hope
Such empty seed should yield a better crop:
Then with both hands I graspt the world together
Thus out of one extream into another: 240
But yet laid hold on virtue seemingly,
Who climbs without hold climbs dangerously:
Be my condition mean, I then take pains
My Family to keep, but not for gains.

A Father I, for children must provide;
But if none, then for kindred near ally'd.
If rich, I'm urged then to gather more,
To bear a port i'th'world, and feed the poor.
If noble, then mine honour to maintain,
If not, riches nobility can gain.   250
For time, for place, likewise for each Relation
I wanted not, my ready allegation.
Yet all my powers for self ends are not spent,
For hundreds bless me for my bounty lent.
Whose backs I've cloth'd, and bellyes I have fed
With mine own fleece, and with my houshold bread,
Yea, justice have I done, was I in place,
To chear the good, and wicked to deface.
The proud I crush't, th'oppressed I set free,
The lyars curb'd, but nourisht verity.   260
Was I a Pastor, I my Flock did feed,
And gently lead the Lambs as they had need.
A Captain I, with Skill I train'd my Band,
And shew'd them how in face of Foes to stand.
A Souldier I, with speed I did obey
As readily, as could my leader say.
Was I a labourer, I wrought all day
As cheerfully as e're I took my pay.
Thus hath mine Age in all sometimes done well,
Sometimes again, mine Age been worse than Hell.   270
In meanness, greatness, riches, poverty,
Did toyle, did broyle, oppress'd, did steal and lye.
Was I as poor as poverty could be,
Then baseness was Companion unto me.
Such scum as hedges and high-ways do yield,
As neither sow, nor reap, nor plant, nor build,
If to Agriculture I was ordain'd,
Great labours, sorrows, Crosses I sustain'd.

The early Cock did summon but in vain
My wakeful thoughts up to my painful gain: 280
My weary Beast rest from his toyle can find,
But if I rest the more distrest my mind.
If happiness my sordidness hath found,
'Twas in the Crop of my manured ground.
My thriving Cattle and my new-milch-Cow,
My fleeced Sheep, and fruitful farrowing Sow:
To greater things I never did aspire,
My dunghil thoughts or hopes could reach no higher.
If to be rich or great it was my fate,
How was I broyl'd with envy and with hate?   290
Greater than was the great'st was my desire,
And thirst for honour, set my heart on fire:
And by Ambition's sails I was so carried,
That over Flats and sands, and Rocks I hurried,
Opprest and sunk, and stav'd all in my way
That did oppose me, to my longed Bay.
My thirst was higher than nobility,
I oft long'd sore to tast on Royalty:
Then Kings must be depos'd or put to flight,
I might possess that Throne which was their right;   300
There set, I rid my self straight out of hand
Of such Competitors, as might in time withstand.
Then thought my state firm founded sure to last,
But in a trice 'tis ruin'd by a blast,
Though cemented with more than noble bloud,
The bottom nought, and so no longer stood.
Sometimes vain glory is the only baite
Whereby my empty Soul is lur'd and caught.
Be I of wit, of learning, and of parts,
I judge I should have room in all mens hearts.   310
And envy gnaws if any do surmount,
I hate, not to be held in high'st account.

If *Bias* like I'm stript unto my skin,
I glory in my wealth I have within.
Thus good and bad, and what I am you see,
Now in a word, what my diseases be.
The vexing stone in bladder and in reins,
The Strangury torments me with sore pains.
The windy Cholick oft my bowels rend,
To break the darksome prison where it's pen'd.   320
The Cramp and Gout doth sadly torture me,
And the restraining, lame Sciatica.
The Astma, Megrim, Palsy, Lethargie,
The quartan Ague, dropsy, Lunacy:
Subject to all distempers (that's the truth)
Though some more incident, to Age or Youth.
And to conclude, I may not tedious be,
Man at his best estate is vanity.

Old Age

What you have been, ev'n such have I before:
And all you say, say I, and somewhat more.   330
Babes innocence, youths wildness I have seen,
And in perplexed middle Age have been:
Sickness, dangers, and anxieties have past,
And on this stage am come to act my last.
I have been young, and strong, and wise as you:
But now *Bis pueri senes*, is too true.
In every Age I've found much vanity,
An end of all perfection now I see.
It's not my valour, honour, nor my gold,
My ruin'd house now falling can uphold.   340
It's not my learning Rhetorick wit so large,
Hath now the power, death's warfare to discharge.
It's not my goodly state, nor bed of downe
That can refresh, or ease, if Conscience frown.

Nor from Alliance can I now have hope,
But what I have done well, that is my prop;
He that in youth is godly, wise and sage,
Provides a staff then to support his Age.
Mutations great, some joyful and some sad,
In this short pilgrimage I oft have had.   350
Sometimes the Heavens with plenty smil'd on me
Sometime again rain'd all Adversity.
Sometimes in honour, sometimes in disgrace,
Sometime an Abject, then again in place.
Such private changes oft mine eyes have seen,
In various times of state I've also been.
I've seen a Kingdome flourish like a tree,
When it was rul'd by that Celestial she;
And like a Cedar, others so surmount:
That but for shrubs they did themselves account.   360
Then saw I *France* and *Holland*, sav'd *Cales* won,
And *Philip* and *Albertus* half undone.
I saw all peace at home, terror to foes,
But ah, I saw at last those eyes to close,
And then methought the day at noon grew dark
When it had lost that radiant Sun-like Spark:
In midst of griefs I saw our hopes revive,
(For 'twas our hopes then kept our hearts alive.)
We chang'd our queen for king under whose rayes
We joy'd in many blest and prosperous dayes.   370
I've seen a Prince, the glory of our land
In prime of youth seiz'd by heavens angry hand,
Which fil'd our hearts with fears, with tears our eyes,
Wailing his fate, and our own destinies.
I've seen from *Rome* an execrable thing,
A Plot to blow up Nobles and their King,
But saw their horrid fact soon disappointed,
And Land and Nobles sav'd with their anointed.

I've Princes seen to live on others lands;
A royal one by gifts from strangers hands   380
Admired for their magnanimity,
Who lost a Prince-dome and a Monarchy.
I've seen designs for *Ree* and *Rochel* crost,
And Poor *Palatinate* for ever lost.
I've seen unworthy men advanced high,
(And better ones suffer extremity)
But neither favour, riches, title, State,
Could length their dayes or once reverse their fate
I've seen one stab'd, and some to loose their heads
And others fly, struck both with gilt and dread.   390
I've seen and so have you, for tis but late,
The desolation of a goodly State,
Plotted and acted so that none can tell,
Who gave the counsel, but the Prince of hell,
Three hundred thousand slaughtered innocents,
By bloudy Popish, hellish miscreants:
Oh may you live, and so you will I trust
To see them swill in bloud untill they burst.
I've seen a King by force thrust from his throne,
And an Usurper subt'ly mount thereon.   400
I've seen a state unmoulded, rent in twain,
But ye may live to see't made up again.
I've seen it plunder'd, taxt and soak'd in bloud,
But out of evill you may see much good.
What are my thoughts, this is no time to say.
Men may more freely speak another day.
These are no old-wives tales, but this is truth,
We old men love to tell what's done in youth.
But I return from whence I stept awry,
My memory is bad, my brain is dry: 410
Mine Almond tree, grey hairs, doe flourish now,
And back once straight, apace begins to bow:

My grinders now are few, my sight doth fail,
My skin is wrinkled, and my cheeks are pale,
No more rejoyce at musicks pleasing noise,
But waking glad to hear the cocks shrill voice:
I cannot scent savours of pleasant meat,
Nor sapors find in what I drink or eat:
My arms and hands once strong have lost their might
I cannot labour, much less can I fight.   420
My comely legs as nimble as the Roe
Now stiff and numb, can hardly creep or goe,
My heart sometimes as fierce as Lion bold,
Now trembling is, all fearful sad and cold;
My golden Bowl and silver Cord e're long
Shall both be broke, by racking death so strong:
Then shall I go whence I shall come no more,
Sons, Nephews, leave my farewel to deplore.
In pleasures and in labours I have found
That Earth can give no consolation sound;   430
To great to rich, to poor, to young, to old,
To mean, to noble, fearful or to bold:
From King to begger, all degrees shall find
But vanity vexation of the mind.
Yea, knowing much, the pleasant'st life of all,
Hath yet among those sweets some bitter gall;
Though reading others works doth much refresh,
Yet studying much brings weariness to th' flesh:
My studies, labours, readings all are done,
And my last period now ev'n almost run.   440
Corruption my Father I do call,
Mother and Sisters both, the worms that crawle
In my dark house, such kindred I have store,
Where I shall rest till heavens shall be no more,
And when this flesh shall rot and be consum'd,
This body by this Soul shall be assum'd:

And I shall see with these same very eyes,
My strong Redeemer coming in the Skies.
Triumph I shall o're sin, o're death, o're Hell,
And in that hope I bid you all farewel.   450

The four Seasons of the Year

Spring

Another four I've left yet to bring on,
Of four times four the last *Quaternion*,
The Winter, Summer, Autumn and the Spring,
In season all these Seasons I shall bring:
Sweet Spring like man in his Minority,
At present claim'd, and had priority.
With smiling face and garments somewhat green,
She trim'd her locks, which late had frosted been,
Nor hot nor cold, she spake, but with a breath,
Fit to revive, the nummed earth from death.   10
Three months (quoth she) are 'lotted to my share
March, *April*, *May* of all the rest most fair.
Tenth of the first, *Sol* into *Aries* enters,
And bids defiance to all tedious winters,
Crosseth the Line, and equals night and day,
(Stil adds to th' last til after pleasant *May*)
And now makes glad the darkned northern wights
Who for some months have seen but starry lights.
Now goes the Plow-man to his merry toyle,
He might unloose his winter locked soyl: 20
The Seeds-man too, doth lavish out his grain,
In hope the more he casts, the more to gain:
The Gardner now superfluous branches lops,
And poles erects for his young clambring hops.

Now digs then sowes his herbs, his flowers and roots
And carefully manures his trees of fruits.
The *Pleiades their influence* now give,
And all that seem'd as dead afresh doth live.
The croaking frogs, whom nipping winter kil'd
Like birds now chirp, and hop about the field,   30
The Nightingale, the black-bird and the Thrush
Now tune their layes, on sprayes of every bush.
The wanton frisking Kid, and soft-fleec'd Lambs
Do jump and play before their feeding Dams,
The tender tops of budding grass they crop,
They joy in what they have, but more in hope:
For though the frost hath lost his binding power,
Yet many a fleece of snow and stormy shower
Doth darken *Sol*'s bright eye, makes us remember
The pinching North-west wind of cold *December*.   40
My second moneth is *April*, green and fair,
Of longer dayes, and a more temperate Air:
The Sun in *Taurus* keeps his residence,
And with his warmer beams glanceth from thence;
This is the month whose fruitful showrs produces
All set and sown for all delights and uses:
The Pear, the Plum, and Apple-tree now flourish
The grass grows long the hungry beast to nourish.
The Primrose pale, and azure violet
Among the virduous grass hath nature set,   50
That when the Sun on's Love (the earth) doth shine
These might as lace set out her garment fine.
The fearfull bird his little house now builds
In trees and walls, in Cities and in fields.
The outside strong, the inside warm and neat;
A natural Artificer compleat.
The clocking hen her chirping chickins leads
With wings and beak defends them from the gleads.

My next and last is fruitfull pleasant *May*,
Wherein the earth is clad in rich aray,   60
The Sun now enters loving *Gemini*,
And heats us with the glances of his eye,
Our thicker rayment makes us lay aside
Lest by his fervor we be torrifi'd.
All flowers the Sun now with his beams discloses,
Except the double pinks and matchless Roses.
Now swarms the busy, witty, honey-Bee,
Whose praise deserves a page from more than me
The cleanly Huswifes Dary's now in th' prime,
Her shelves and firkins fill'd for winter time.   70
The meads with Cowslips, Honey-suckles dight,
One hangs his head, the other stands upright:
But both rejoyce at th' heavens clear smiling face,
More at her showers, which water them a space.
For fruits my Season yields the early Cherry,
The hasty Peas, and wholsome cool Strawberry.
More solid fruits require a longer time,
Each Season hath his fruit, so hath each Clime:
Each man his own peculiar excellence,
But none in all that hath preheminence.   80
Sweet fragrant Spring, with thy short pittance fly
Let some describe thee better than can I.
Yet above all this priviledg is thine,
Thy dayes still lengthen without least decline.

    Summer

When *Spring* had done, the *Summer* did begin,
With melted tauny face, and garments thin,
Resembling Fire, Choler, and Middle age,
As *Spring* did Air, Blood, Youth in's equipage.

Wiping the sweat from off her face that ran,
With hair all wet she puffing thus began; 90
Bright *June*, *July* and *August* hot are mine,
In'th first *Sol* doth in crabbed *Cancer* shine.
His progress to the North now's fully done,
Then retrograde must be my burning Sun,
Who to his southward Tropick still is bent,
Yet doth his parching heat but more augment
Though he decline, because his flames so fair,
Have throughly dry'd the earth, and heat the air.
Like as an Oven that long time hath been heat,
Whose vehemency at length doth grow so great, 100
That if you do withdraw her burning store,
Tis for a time as fervent as before.
Now go those frolick Swains, the shepheard lad,
To wash the thick cloth'd flocks with pipes full glad
In the cool streams they labour with delight
Rubbing their dirty coats till they look white:
Whose fleece when finely spun and deeply dy'd
With Robes thereof Kings have been dignifi'd.
Blest rustick Swains, your pleasant quiet life,
Hath envy bred in Kings that were at strife, 110
Careless of worldly wealth you sing and pipe,
Whilst they'r imbroyl'd in wars and troubles rife:
Which made great *Bajazet* cry out in's woes,
Oh happy shepherd which hath not to lose
Orthobulus, nor yet *Sebastia* great,
But whist'leth to thy flock in cold and heat.
Viewing the Sun by day, the Moon by night
Endimions, *Dianaes* dear delight,
Upon the grass resting your healthy limbs,
By purling Brooks looking how fishes swims. 120
If pride within your lowly Cells ere haunt,
Of him that was Shepherd then King go vaunt.

This moneth the Roses are distil'd in glasses,
Whose fragrant smel all made perfumes surpasses;
The Cherry, Gooseberry are now in th' prime,
And for all sorts of Pease, this is the time.
July my next, the hott'st in all the year,
The sun through *Leo* now takes his Career,
Whose flaming breath doth melt us from afar,
Increased by the star Canicular.   130
This Month from *Julius Cæsar* took its name,
By Romans celebrated to his fame.
Now go the Mowers to their slashing toyle,
The Meadowes of their riches to dispoyle,
With weary strokes, they take all in their way,
Bearing the burning heat of the long day.
The forks and Rakes do follow them amain,
Which makes the aged fields look young again.
The groaning Carts do bear away this prize,
To Stacks and Barns where it for Fodder lyes.   140
My next and last is *August* fiery hot
(For much, the *Southward* Sun abateth not)
This Moneth he keeps with *Virgo* for a space,
The dryed Earth is parched with his face.
August of great *Augustus* took its name,
Romes second Emperour of lasting fame,
With sickles now the bending Reapers goe
The russling tress of *terra* down to mowe;
And bundles up in sheaves, the weighty wheat,
Which after Manchet makes for Kings to eat: 150
The Barly, Rye and Pease should first had place,
Although their bread have not so white a face.
The Carter leads all home with whistling voyce,
He plow'd with pain, but reaping doth rejoyce;
His sweat, his toyle, his careful wakeful nights,
His fruitful Crop abundantly requites.

Now's ripe the Pear, Pear-plumb, and Apricock,
The prince of plumbs, whose stone's as hard as Rock.
The Summer seems but short, the Autumn hasts
To shake his fruits, of most delicious tasts   160
Like good old Age, whose younger juicy Roots
Hath still ascended, to bear goodly fruits.
Until his head be gray, and strength be gone.
Yet then appears the worthy deeds he'th done:
To feed his boughs exhausted hath his sap,
Then drops his fruits into the eaters lap.

Autumn

Of *Autumn* moneths *September* is the prime,
Now day and night are equal in each Clime,
The twelfth of this *Sol* riseth in the Line,
And doth in poizing *Libra* this month shine.   170
The vintage now is ripe, the grapes are prest,
Whose lively liquor oft is curs'd and blest:
For nought so good, but it may be abused,
But its a precious juice when well its used.
The raisins now in clusters dryed be,
The Orange, Lemon dangle on the tree:
The Pomegranate, the Fig are ripe also,
And Apples now their yellow sides do show.
Of Almonds, Quinces, Wardens, and of Peach,
The season's now at hand of all and each.   180
Sure at this time, time first of all began,
And in this moneth was made apostate Man:
For then in *Eden* was not only seen,
Boughs full of leaves, or fruits unripe or green,
Or withered stocks, which were all dry and dead,
But trees with goodly fruits replenished;
Which shews nor Summer, Winter nor the Spring

Our Grand-Sire was of Paradice made King:
Nor could that temp'rate Clime such difference make,
If scited as the most Judicious take.   190
October is my next, we hear in this
The Northern winter-blasts begin to hiss.
In *Scorpio* resideth now the Sun,
And his declining heat is almost done.
The fruitless Trees all withered now do stand,
Whose sapless yellow leavs, by winds are fan'd,
Which notes when youth and strength have past their
                prime
Decrepit age must also have its time.
The Sap doth slily creep towards the Earth
There rests, until the Sun give it a birth.   200
So doth old Age still tend unto his grave,
Where also he his winter time must have;
But when the Sun of righteousness draws nigh,
His dead old stock, shall mount again on high.
November is my last, for Time doth haste,
We now of winters sharpness 'gins to tast.
This moneth the Sun's in *Sagitarius*,
So farre remote, his glances warm not us.
Almost at shortest is the shorten'd day,
The *Northern* pole beholdeth not one ray.   210
Now *Greenland, Groanland, Finland, Lapland,* see
No Sun, to lighten their obscurity:
Poor wretches that in total darkness lye,
With minds more dark than is the dark'ned Sky.
Beaf, Brawn, and Pork are now in great request,
And solid meats our stomacks can digest.
This time warm cloaths, full diet, and good fires,
Our pinched flesh, and hungry mawes requires:
Old, cold, dry Age and Earth *Autumn* resembles,
And Melancholy which most of all dissembles.   220

I must be short, and shorts, the short'ned day,
What winter hath to tell, now let him say.

    Winter

Cold, moist, young flegmy winter now doth lye
In swadling Clouts, like new born Infancy
Bound up with frosts, and furr'd with hail and snows,
And like an Infant, still it taller grows;
December is my first, and now the Sun
To th' Southward *Tropick*, his swift race doth run:
This moneth he's hous'd in horned *Capricorn*,
From thence he 'gins to length the shortned morn,   230
Through *Christendome* with great Feastivity,
Now's held, (but ghest) for blest Nativity.
Cold frozen *January* next comes in,
Chilling the blood and shrinking up the skin;
In *Aquarius* now keeps the long wisht Sun,
And Northward his unwearied Course doth run:
The day much longer than it was before,
The cold not lessened, but augmented more.
Now Toes and Ears, and Fingers often freeze,
And Travellers their noses sometimes leese.   240
Moist snowie *February* is my last,
I care not how the winter time doth haste.
In *Pisces* now the golden Sun doth shine,
And Northward still approaches to the Line,
The Rivers 'gin to ope, the snows to melt,
And some warm glances from his face are felt;
Which is increased by the lengthen'd day,
Until by's heat, he drive all cold away,
And thus the year in Circle runneth round:
Where first it did begin, in th' end its found.   250

My Subjects bare, my Brain is bad,
Or better Lines you should have had:
The first fell in so nat'rally,
I knew not how to pass it by;
The last, though bad I could not mend,
Accept therefore of what is pen'd,
And all the faults that you shall spy
Shall at your feet for pardon cry.

The four Monarchyes, the Assyrian being the first, beginning under Nimrod, 131. Years after the Flood

When time was young, and World in Infancy,
Man did not proudly strive for Soveraignty:
But each one thought his petty Rule was high,
If of his house he held the Monarchy.
This was the golden Age, but after came
The boisterous son of *Cush,* Grand-Child to *Ham,*
That mighty Hunter, who in his strong toyles
Both Beasts and Men subjected to his spoyles:
The strong foundation of proud *Babel* laid,
Erech, Accad, and *Culneh* also made.   10
These were his first, all stood in *Shinar* land,
From thence he went *Assyria* to command,
And mighty *Niniveh,* he there begun,
Not finished till he his race had run.
Resen, Caleh, and *Rehoboth* likewise
By him to Cities eminent did rise.
Of *Saturn,* he was the Original,
Whom the succeeding times a God did call,
When thus with rule, he had been dignifi'd,
One hundred fourteen years he after dy'd.   20

Unworthy *Belshazzar* next wears the crown,
Whose acts profane a sacred Pen sets down,
His lust and crueltyes in storyes find,
A royal State ruled by a bruitish mind.
His life so base, and dissolute invites
The noble *Persian* to invade his rights.
Who with his own, and Uncles power anon,
Layes siedge to's Regal Seat, proud *Babylon*,
The coward King, whose strength lay in his walls,
To banquetting and revelling now falls,   30
To shew his little dread, but greater store,
To chear his friends, and scorn his foes the more.
The holy vessels thither brought long since,
They carrows'd in, and sacrilegious prince
Did praise his Gods of mettal, wood, and stone,
Protectors of his Crown, and *Babylon*,
But he above, his doings did deride,
And with a hand soon dashed all this pride.
The King upon the wall casting his eye,
The fingers of a hand writing did spy,   40
Which horrid sight, he fears must needs portend
Destruction to his Crown, to's Person end.
With quaking knees, and heart appall'd he cries,
For the Soothsayers, and Magicians wise;
This language strange to read, and to unfold;
With gifts of Scarlet robe, and Chain of gold,
And highest dignity, next to the King,
To him that could interpret, clear this thing:
But dumb the gazing Astrologers stand,
Amazed at the writing, and the hand.   50
None answers the affrighted Kings intent,
Who still expects some fearful sad event;

As dead, alive he sits, as one undone:
In comes the Queen, to chear her heartless Son.
Of *Daniel* tells, who in his grand-sires dayes
Was held in more account than now he was.
Daniel in haste is brought before the King,
Who doth not flatter, nor once cloak the thing;
Reminds him of his Grand-Sires height and fall,
And of his own notorious sins withall: 60
His Drunkenness, and his profaness high,
His pride and sottish gross Idolatry.
The guilty King with colour pale and dead
Then hears his *Mene* and his *Tekel* read.
And one thing did worthy a King (though late)
Perform'd his word to him that told his fate.
That night victorious *Cyrus* took the town,
Who soon did terminate his life and crown;
With him did end the race of *Baladan:*
And now the *Persian* Monarchy began.   70

An Apology

To finish what's begun, was my intent,
My thoughts and my endeavours thereto bent;
Essays I many made but still gave out,
The more I mus'd, the more I was in doubt:
The subject large, my mind and body weak,
With many moe discouragements did speak.
All thoughts of further progress laid aside,
Though oft perswaded, I as oft deny'd,
At length resolv'd, when many years had past,
To prosecute my story to the last;   80
And for the same, I hours not few did spend,
And weary lines (though lanke) I many pen'd:
But 'fore I could accomplish my desire,

My papers fell a prey to th' raging fire.
And thus my pains (with better things) I lost,
Which none had cause to wail, nor I to boast.
No more I'le do sith I have suffer'd wrack,
Although my Monarchies their legs do lack:
Nor matter is't this last, the world now sees,
Hath many Ages been upon his knees.   90

APPENDIX A

My dear Children,—

I knowing by experience that the exhortations of parents take most effect when the speakers leave to speak, and those especially sink deepest which are spoke latest — and being ignorant whether on my death bed I shall have opportunity to speak to any of you, much lesse to All — thought it the best, whilst I was able to compose some short matters, (for what else to call them I know not) and bequeath to you, that when I am no more with you, yet I may bee dayly in your remembrance, (Although that is the least in my aim in what I now doe) but that you may gain some spiritual Advantage by my experience. I have not studied in this you read to show my skill, but to declare the Truth — not to sett forth myself, but the Glory of God. If I had minded the former, it had been perhaps better pleasing to you, — but seing the last is the best, let it bee best pleasing to you.

The method I will observe shall bee this — I will begin with God's dealing with me from my childhood to this Day. In my young years, about 6 or 7 as I take it, I began to make conscience of my wayes, and what I knew was sinfull, as lying, disobedience to Parents, &c. I avoided it. If at any time I was overtaken with the like evills, it was a great Trouble. I could not be at rest 'till by prayer I had confest it unto God. I was also troubled at the neglect of Private Dutyes, tho' too often tardy that way. I also found much comfort in reading the Scriptures, especially those places I thought most concerned my Condition, and as I grew to have more understanding, so the more solace I took in them.

In a long fitt of sicknes which I had on my bed I often communed with my heart, and made my supplication to the most High who sett me free from that affliction.

But as I grew up to bee about 14 or 15 I found my heart more carnall, and sitting loose from God, vanity and the follyes of youth take hold of me.

About 16, the Lord layd his hand sore upon me and smott mee with the small pox. When I was in my affliction, I besought the Lord, and confessed my Pride and Vanity and he was entreated of me, and again restored me. But I rendered not to him according to the benefitt received.

After a short time I changed my condition and was marryed, and came into this Country, where I found a new world and new manners, at which my heart rose. But after I was convinced it was the way of God, I submitted to it and joined to the church at Boston.

After some time I fell into a lingering sicknes like a consumption, together with a lamenesse, which correction I saw the Lord sent to humble and try me and doe mee Good: and it was not altogether ineffectuall.

It pleased God to keep me a long time without a child, which was a great greif to me, and cost mee many prayers and tears before I obtaind one, and after him gave mee many more, of whom I now take the care, that as I have brought you into the world, and with great paines, weaknes, cares, and feares brought you to this, I now travail in birth again of you till Christ bee formed in you.

Among all my experiences of God's gratious Dealings with me I have constantly observed this, that he hath never suffered me long to sitt loose from him, but by one affliction or other hath made me look home, and search what was amisse — so usually thus it hath been with me that I have no sooner felt my heart out of order, but I have expected correction for it, which most commonly hath been upon my own person, in sicknesse, weaknes, paines, sometimes on my soul, in Doubts and feares of God's displeasure, and my sincerity towards him, sometimes he hath smott a child with sicknes, sometimes chasstened by losses in estate, — and these Times (thro' his great mercy) have been the times of my greatest Getting and Advantage, yea I have found them the Times when the Lord hath manifested the most Love to me. Then have I gone to searching, and have said with David, Lord search me and try me, see what wayes of wickednes are in me, and lead me in the way everlasting: and seldome or never but I have found either some sin I lay under which God would have reformed, or some duty neglected which he would have performed. And by his help I have layd Vowes and Bonds upon my Soul to perform his righteous commands.

If at any time you are chastened of God, take it as thankfully and Joyfully as in greatest mercyes, for if yee bee his yee shall reap the greatest benefitt by it. It hath been no small support to me in times of Darknes when the Almighty hath hid his face from me, that yet I have had abundance of sweetnes and refreshment after affliction, and more circumspection in my walking after I have been afflicted. I have been with God like an untoward child, that no longer than the rod has been on my back (or at least in sight) but I have been apt to forgett him and myself too. Before I was afflicted I went astray, but now I keep the statutes.

I have had great experience of God's hearing my Prayers, and returning comfortable Answers to me, either in granting the Thing I prayed for, or else in satisfying my mind without it; and I have been confident it hath been from him, because I have found my heart through his goodnes enlarged in Thankfullnes to him.

I have often been perplexed that I have not found that constant Joy in my Pilgrimage and refreshing which I supposed most of the servants of God have; although he hath not left me altogether without the wittnes of his holy spirit, who hath oft given mee his word and sett to his Seal that it shall bee well with me. I have som-times tasted of that hidden Manna that the world knowes not, and have sett up my Ebenezer, and have resolved with myself that against such a promis, such tasts of sweetnes, the Gates of Hell shall never prevail. Yet have I many Times sinkings and droopings, and not enjoyed that felicity that somtimes I have done. But when I have been in darknes and seen no light, yet have I desired to stay my self upon the Lord.

And, when I have been in sicknes and pain, I have thought if the Lord would but lift up the light of his Countenance upon me, altho' he ground me to powder, it would bee but light to me; yea, oft have I thought were it hell itself, and could there find the Love of God toward me, it would bee a Heaven. And, could I have been in Heaven without the Love of God, it would have been a Hell to me; for, in Truth, it is the absence and presence of God that makes Heaven or Hell.

Many times hath Satan troubled me concerning the verity of the scriptures, many times by Atheisme how I could know whether there was a God; I never saw any miracles to confirm me, and those which I read of how did I know but they were feigned. That there is a God my Reason would soon tell me by the wondrous workes that I see, the vast frame of the Heaven and the Earth, the order of all things, night and day, Summer and Winter, Spring and Autumne, the dayly providing for this great houshold upon the Earth, the preserving and directing of All to its proper end. The consideration of these things would with amazement certainly resolve me that there is an Eternall Being.

But how should I know he is such a God as I worship in Trinity, and such a Saviour as I rely upon? tho' this hath thousands of Times been suggested to mee, yet God hath helped me over. I have argued thus with myself. That there is a God I see. If ever this God hath revealed himself, it must bee in his word, and this must bee it or none. Have I not found that operation by it that no humane Invention can work upon the Soul? hath not Judgments befallen Diverse who have scorned and contemd it? hath it not been preserved thro' All Ages maugre all the heathen Tyrants and all of the enemyes who have opposed it? Is there any story but that which showes the beginnings of Times, and how the world came to bee as wee see? Doe wee not know the prophecyes in it fullfilled which could not have been so long foretold by any but God himself?

When I have gott over this Block, then have I another putt in my way, That admitt this bee the true God whom wee worship, and that bee his word, yet why may not the Popish Religion bee the right? They have the same God, the same Christ, the same word: they only enterprett it one way, wee another.

This hath somtimes stuck with me, and more it would, but the vain fooleries that are in their Religion, together with their lying miracles and cruell persecutions of the Saints, which admitt were they as they terme them, yet not so to bee dealt withall.

182   APPENDIX A

The consideration of these things and many the like would soon turn me to my own Religion again.

But some new Troubles I have had since the world has been filled with Blasphemy, and Sectaries, and some who have been accounted sincere Christians have been carried away with them, that somtimes I have said, Is there Faith upon the earth? and I have not known what to think. But then I have remembred the words of Christ that so it must bee, and that, if it were possible, the very elect should bee deceived. Behold, saith our Saviour, I have told you before. That hath stayed my heart, and I can now say, Return, O my Soul, to thy Rest, upon this Rock Christ Jesus will I build my faith; and, if I perish, I perish. But I know all the Powers of Hell shall never prevail against it. I know whom I have trusted, and whom I have beleived, and that he is able to keep that I have committed to his charge.

Now to the King, Immortall, Eternall, and invisible, the only wise God, bee Honoure and Glory for ever and ever! Amen.

This was written in much sicknesse and weaknes, and is very weakly and imperfectly done; but, if you can pick any Benefitt out of it, it is the marke which I aimed at.

July 8th, 1656.

I had a sore fitt of fainting, which lasted 2 or 3 dayes, but not in that extremity which at first it took me, and so much the sorer it was to me because my dear husband was from home (who is my cheifest comforter on Earth); but my God, who never failed me, was not absent, but helped me, and gratiously manifested his Love to me, which I dare not passe by without Remembrance, that it may bee a support to me when I shall have occasion to read this hereafter, and to others that shall read it when I shall possesse that I now hope for, that so they may bee encouragd to trust in him who is the only Portion of his Servants.

O Lord, let me never forgett thy Goodnes, nor question thy faithfullnes to me, for thou art my God: Thou hast said, and shall not I beleive it?

Thou hast given me a pledge of that Inheritance thou hast promised to bestow upon me. O, never let Satan prevail against me, but strengthen my faith in Thee, 'till I shall attain the end of my hopes, even the Salvation of my Soul. Come, Lord Jesus; come quickly.

August 28, 1656.

After much weaknes and sicknes when my spirits were worn out, and many times my faith weak likewise, the Lord was pleased to uphold my drooping heart, and to manifest his Love to me; and this is that which stayes my Soul that this condition that I am in is the best for me, for God doth not afflict willingly, nor take delight in greiving the children of men: he hath no benefitt by my adversity, nor is he the better for my prosperity; but he doth it for my Advantage, and that I may bee a Gainer by it. And if he knowes that weaknes and a frail body is the best to make me a vessell fitt for his use, why should I not bare it, not only willingly but joyfully? The Lord knowes I dare not desire that health that somtimes I have had, least my heart should bee drawn from him, and sett upon the world.

Now I can wait, looking every day when my Saviour shall call for me. Lord graunt that while I live I may doe that service I am able in this frail Body, and bee in continuall expectation of my change, and let me never forgett thy great Love to my soul so lately expressed, when I could lye down and bequeath my Soul to thee, and Death seem'd no terrible Thing. O let me ever see Thee that Art invisible, and I shall not bee unwilling to come, tho' by so rough a Messenger.

May 11, 1657.

I had a sore sicknes, and weaknes took hold of me, which hath by fitts lasted all this Spring till this 11 May, yet hath my God given me many a respite, and some ability to perform the Dutyes I owe to him, and the work of my famely.

Many a refreshment have I found in this my weary Pilgrimage, and in this valley of Baca many pools of water. That which now I cheifly labour for is a contented, thankfull heart under my affliction and weaknes, seing it is the will of God it should bee thus. Who am I that I should repine at his pleasure, especially seing it is for my spirituall advantage? for I hope my soul shall flourish while my body decayes, and the weaknes of this outward man shall bee a meanes to strenghten my inner man.

Yet a little while and he that shall come will come, and will not tarry.

Sept. 30, 1657.

It pleased God to viset me with my old Distemper of weaknes and fainting, but not in that sore manner somtimes he hath. I desire not only willingly, but thankfully, to submitt to him, for I trust it is out of his abundant Love to my straying Soul which in prosperity is too much in love with the world. I have found by experience I can no more live without correction than without food. Lord, with thy correction give Instruction and amendment, and then thy stroakes shall bee welcome. I have not been refined in the furnace of affliction as some have been, but have rather been preserved with sugar than brine, yet will he preserve me to his heavenly kingdom.

Thus (dear children) have yee seen the many sicknesses and weaknesses that I have passed thro' to the end that, if you meet with the like, you may have recourse to the same God who hath heard and delivered me, and will doe the like for you if you trust in him; And, when he shall deliver you out of distresse, forget not to give him thankes, but to walk more closely with him than before. This is the desire of your Loving mother,   A. B.

May 11, 1661.

It hath pleased God to give me a long Time of respite for these 4 years that I have had no great fitt of sickness, but this year, from the middle of January 'till May, I have been by fitts very ill and weak. The first of this month I had a feaver seat'd upon me which, indeed, was the longest and sorest that ever I had, lasting 4 dayes, and the weather being very hott made it the more tedious, but it pleased the Lord to support my heart in his goodnes, and to hear my Prayers, and to deliver me out of adversity. But, alas! I cannot render unto the Lord according to all his loving kindnes, nor take the cup of salvation with Thanksgiving as I ought to doe. Lord, Thou that knowest All things know'st that I desire to testefye my thankfullnes not only in word, but in Deed, that my Conversation may speak that thy vowes are upon me.

For my deare sonne Simon Bradstreet

Parents perpetuate their lives in their posterity, and their maners in their imitation. Children do natureally rather follow the failings than the vertues of their predecessors, but I am perswaded better things of you. You once desired me to leave something for you in writeing that you might look upon when you should see me no more. I could think of nothing more fit for you, nor of more ease to my self than these short meditations following. Such as they are I bequeath to you: small legacys are accepted by true friends, much more by duty full children. I have avoyded incroaching upon other conceptions because I would leave you nothing but myne owne, though in value they fall short of all in this kinde, yet I presume they will be better pris'd by you for the Authors sake. the Lord blesse you with grace heer, and crown you with glory heerafter, that I may meet you with rejoyceing at that great day of appearing, which is the continuall prayer, of your affectionate mother,
March 20, 1664.   A. B.

APPENDIX B

Meditations Divine and morall (Selection)

1

There is no object that we see; no action that we doe; no good that we injoy; no evill that we feele, or fear, but we may make some spirituall advantage of all: and he that makes such improvment is wise, as well as pious.

2

Many can speak well, but few can do well. We are better scholars in the Theory than the practique part, but he is a true Christian that is a proficient in both.   •

3

Youth is the time of getting, middle age of improving, and old age of spending; a negligent youth is usually attended by an ignorant middle age, and both by an empty old age. He that hath nothing to feed on but vanity and lyes must needs lye down in the Bed of sorrow.

4

A ship that beares much saile, and little or no ballast, is easily overset, and that man, whose head hath great abilities, and his heart little or no grace, is in danger of foundering.

5

It is reported of the peakcock that, prideing himself in his gay feathers, he ruffles them up; but, spying his black feet, he soon lets fall his plumes, so he that glorys in his gifts and adornings, should look upon his Corruptions, and that will damp his high thoughts.

6

The finest bread hath the least bran; the purest hony, the least wax; and the sincerest christian, the least self love.

7

The hireling that labours all the day, comforts himself that when night comes he shall both take his rest, and receive his reward; the painfull christian that hath wrought hard in Gods vineyard, and hath born the heat and drought of the day, when he perceives his sun apace to decline, and the shadowes of his evening to be stretched out, lifts up his head with joy, knowing his refreshing is at hand.

8

Downny beds make drosey persons, but hard lodging keeps the eyes open. A prosperous state makes a secure Christian, but adversity makes him Consider.

9

Sweet words are like hony, a little may refresh, but too much gluts the stomach.

10

Diverse children have their different natures; some are like flesh which nothing but salt will keep from putrefaction; some again like tender fruits that are best preserved with sugar: those parents are wise that can fit their nurture according to their Nature.

11

That town which thousands of enemys without hath not been able to take, hath been delivered up by one traytor within; and that man, which all the temptations of Sathan without could not hurt, hath been foild by one lust within.

12

Authority without wisedome is like a heavy axe without an edg, fitter to bruise than polish.

13

The reason why christians are so loth to exchang this world for a better, is because they have more sence than faith: they se what they injoy, they do but hope for that which is to Come.

14

If we had no winter the spring would not be so pleasant: if we did not sometimes tast of adversity, prosperity would not be so welcome.

15

A low man can goe upright under that door, wher a taller is glad to stoop; so a man of weak faith and mean abilities, may undergo a crosse more patiently than he that excells him, both in gifts and graces.

16

That house which is not often swept, makes the cleanly inhabitant soone loath it, and that heart which is not continually purifieing it self, is no fit temple for the spirit of god to dwell in.

17

Few men are so humble as not to be proud of their abilitys; and nothing will abase them more than this, — what hast thou, but what thou hast received? come give an account of thy stewardship.

18

He that will untertake to climb up a steep mountain with a great burden on his back, will finde it a wearysome, if not an impossible task; so he that thinkes to mount to heaven clog'd with the Cares and riches of this Life, 'tis no wonder if he faint by the way.

Corne, till it have past through the Mill and been ground to powder, is not fit for bread. God so deales with his servants: he grindes them with greif and pain till they turn to dust, and then are they fit manchet for his Mansion.

23

The skillfull fisher hath his severall baits for severall fish, but there is a hooke under all; Satan, that great Angler, hath his sundry baits for sundry tempers of men, which they all catch gredily at, but few perceives the hook till it be to late.

25

An akeing head requires a soft pillow; and a drooping heart a strong support.

26

A sore finger may disquiet the whole body, but an ulcer within destroys it: so an enemy without may disturb a Commonwealth, but dissentions within over throw it.

27

It is a pleasant thing to behold the light, but sore eyes are not able to look upon it; the pure in heart shall se God, but the defiled in conscience shall rather choose to be buried under rocks and mountains than to behold the presence of the Lamb.

28

Wisedome with an inheritance is good, but wisedome without an inheritance is better than an inheritance without wisedome.

30

Yellow leaves argue want of sap, and gray haires want of moisture;

so dry and saplesse performances are simptoms of little spiritall vigor.

31

Iron till it be throughly heat is uncapable to be wrought; so God sees good to cast some men into the furnace of affliction, and then beats them on his anvile into what frame he pleases.

32

Ambitious men are like hops that never rest climbing soe long as they have any thing to stay upon; but take away their props and they are, of all, the most dejected.

34

Dimne eyes are the concomitants of old age; and short sightednes, in those that are eyes of a Republique, foretels a declineing State.

35

We read in Scripture of three sorts of Arrows, — the arrow of an enemy, the arrow of pestilence, and the arrow of a slanderous tongue; the two first kill the body, the last the good name; the two former leave a man when he is once dead, but the last mangles him in his grave.

36

Sore labourers have hard hands, and old sinners have brawnie Consciences.

38

Some Children are hardly weaned, although the teat be rub'd with wormwood or mustard, they wil either wipe it off, or else suck down sweet and bitter together; so it is with some Christians, let God imbitter all the sweets of this life, that so they might feed upon more substantiall food, yet they are so childishly sottish that they are still huging and sucking these empty brests, that God is forced to hedg up their way with thornes, or lay affliction on their loynes, that so they might shake hands with the world before it bid them farwell.

45

We often se stones hang with drops, not from any innate moisture, but from a thick ayre about them; so may we sometime se marble hearted sinners seem full of contrition, but it is not from any dew of grace within, but from some black Clouds that impends them, which produces these sweating effects.

49

The treasures of this world may well be compared to huskes, for they have no kernell in them, and they that feed upon them, may soon stuffe their throats, but cannot fill their bellys; they may be choaked by them, but cannot be satisfied with them.

50

Somtimes the sun is only shadowed by a cloud that wee cannot se his luster, although we may walk by his light, but when he is set we are in darknes till he arise againe; so God doth somtime vaile his face but for a moment, that we cannot behold the light of his Countenance as at some other time, yet he affords so much light as may direct our way, that we may go forwards to the Citty of habitation, but when he seemes to set and be quite gone out of sight, then must we needs walk in darknesse and se no light, yet then must we trust in the Lord, and stay upon our God, and when the morning (which is the appointed time) is come, the Sun of righteousnes will arise with healing in his wings.

53

He that is to saile into a farre country, although the ship, cabbin, and provision, be all convenient and comfortable for him, yet he hath no desire to make that his place of residence, but longs to put in at that port wher his bussines lyes: a christian is sailing through this world unto his heavenly country, and heere he hath many conveniences and comforts but he must beware of desireing to make this the place of his abode, lest he meet with such tossings that may cause him to long for shore before he sees land. We must, therefore, be heer as strangers and pilgrims, that we may plainly declare that we seek a citty above, and wait all the dayes of our appointed time till our chang shall come.

55

We read of ten lepers that were Cleansed, but of one that returned thanks: we are more ready to receive mercys than we are to acknowledg them: men can use great importunity when they are in distresses, and shew great ingratitude after their successes; but he that ordereth his conversation aright, will glorifie him that heard him in the day of his trouble.

61

Corne is produced with much labour (as the husbandman well knowes), and some land askes much more paines than some other doth to be brought into tilth, yet all must be ploughed and harrowed; some children (like sowre land) are of so tough and morose a disposition, that the plough of correction must make long furrows on their back, and the Harrow of discipline goe often over them, before they bee fit soile to sow the seed of morality, much lesse of grace in them. But when by prudent nurture they are brought into a fit capacity, let the seed of good instruction and exhortation be sown in the spring of their youth, and a plentifull crop may be expected in the harvest of their yeares.

62

As man is called the little world, so his heart may be cal'd the little Commonwealth: his more fixed and resolved thoughts are like to inhabitants, his slight and flitting thoughts are like passengers that travell to and fro continually; here is also the great Court of justice erected, which is alway kept by conscience who is both accuser, excuser, witnes, and Judg, whom no bribes can pervert, nor flattery cause to favour, but as he finds the evidence, so he absolves or condemnes: yea, so Absolute is this Court of Judicature, that there is no appeale from it, — no, not to the Court of heaven itself, — for if our conscience condemn us, he, also, who is greater than our conscience, will do it much more; but he that would have boldnes to go to the throne of grace to be accepted there, must be sure to carry a certificate from the Court of conscience, that he stands right there.

77

God hath by his providence so ordered, that no one Country hath all Commoditys within it self, but what it wants, another shall supply, that so there may be a mutuall Commerce through the world. As it is with Countrys so it is with men, there was never yet any one man that had all excellences, let his parts, naturall and acquired, spirituall and morall, be never so large, yet he stands in need of something which another man hath, (perhaps meaner than himself,) which shews us perfection is not below, as also, that God will have us beholden one to another.

NOTES

The abbreviations *T* and *E* used in these notes refer to material quoted from one of the following editions:

T = *The Tenth Muse*, London, 1650.

E = *The Works of Anne Bradstreet in Prose and Verse*, edited by John Harvard Ellis, Cambridge, Mass., 1867 (based on *Several Poems*, Boston, 1678). See Bibliography.

Since *E* is followed for the most part in the text, *T* indicates interesting variations to be found in *The Tenth Muse*.

All material in roman (ordinary) type may be assumed to be the work of Anne Bradstreet; all explanatory material in *italics* is that of the editor.

Words or phrases following a *colon* are the editor's suggested interpretations; words or phrases following a *bracket* represent textual variations from one edition to the next.

Some copies of the 1678 edition of *Several Poems*, including that at the New York Public Library, contain an errata leaf. Corrections marked "errata leaf" represent readings taken from this source.

In the prose Meditations (Appendix B), Buchanan Charles has pointed out certain discrepancies between Ellis's readings and those in the small manuscript book at the Stevens Memorial Library, North Andover, Mass. These discrepancies are labeled "BC."

I am indebted in all these Notes, even when I have sometimes failed to credit him, to the excellent scholarship of John Harvard Ellis.

The Author to Her Book

This poem, from the second (1678) edition, expresses the author's embarrassment at the appearance of " The Tenth Muse . . .," the manuscript of which had been taken to England by her brother-in-law and published without her knowledge. See Introduction, p. 9.

18. find.] find *E*

To my Dear and loving Husband

This and the following four poems were not, of course, intended by the author for publication; they are preceded in the 1678 edition by the editor's statement: Several other Poems made by the Author upon Diverse Occasions, were found among her Papers after her Death, which she never meant should come to publick view; amongst which, these following (at the desire of some friends that knew her well) are here inserted.

11. lets: *let's.*

"*As loving Hind*"

The concluding couplet is signed "*A.B.*" in Ellis. See Introduction and notes to " *Upon my dear and loving husband his goeing into England,*" below, for explanations of her husband's frequent official absences from home.

6. this,] this. *E*
15. wooes: *woo.*
22. phere: *fere (consort or spouse).* Campbell changes to "living sphere." Hensley has "peer."
29. brouze: *browse, nibble.*

"*Phœbus make haste*"

5. drown'd: *drown out.* drown'd] drown'd) *E*
6. sound),] sound, *E*
10. widdowed: *temporarily abandoned.*
11. brakish: *salty.*

A Letter to her Husband

Signed "*A.B.*" in Ellis; the title is Ellis's.

7. I like the earth: *I, like the earth.*
21. Cancer: (*the zodiacal sign is meant*).

Before the Birth of one of her Children

Signed "*A.B.*" in Ellis; the title is Ellis's.

5. irrevocable] irrovocable *E*
11. unty'd] unty d *E*

16. oblivious *errata leaf*] oblivions *E*

24. step Dames: *stepdame's.*

In reference to her Children, 23. June, 1656

Signed " A.B." in Ellis, who suggests that " 1656" may be a misprint for 1658, since later events are referred to. The poem is moved forward from its normal position in this section since it, more than any other, offers an introduction to members of her family. See also the poems in Section III *dealing with her husband, her son Samuel, and her daughter Hannah.*

  5. wing,] wing. *E*

  7. Chief of the Brood . . . flight: *Samuel Bradstreet sailed for England in 1657 and returned to New England in 1661.*

 13. My second bird: *Dorothy, who married the Rev. Seaborn Cotton in 1654, accompanying him to Wethersfield, Conn., and later to Hampton, N.H.*

 18. steer'd] steer d *E*

 20. treen: *trees.*

 21. I have a third: *Sarah, who married Richard Hubbard of Ipswich.*

 27. One to the Academy: *Simon Bradstreet, who entered Harvard June 25, 1656.*

 33. My fifth: *Ellis suggests this is a misprint for seventh, referring to her son Dudley.*

 37. My other three: *her children Hannah, Mercy, and John, still at home at the time of writing.*

 51. least: *lest.*

Upon a Fit of Sickness

This poem and the following one, together with " Upon some distemper of body" and the four poems expressing grief at the deaths of grandchildren and her daughter-in-law, were found among Mrs. Bradstreet's papers at her death, and were not intended for publication.

To her Father with some verses

Signed " A.B." in Ellis.

  5. principle: *principal.*

 10. loose: *lose.*   right.] right *E*

To the Memory of my . . . Father

    6. ought: *owed.*

  11. knaw: *gnaw.*

  13. lead: *led.*

  14. procure,] procure. *E*

  29. Truths: *Truth's.*

  30. maligne so: (*the meter suggests that the word "thee" may have been omitted after "maligne"*).

  32. Fathers: *Father's.*

  35. High: *proud.*

  69. others: *other's.*

On my dear and ever honoured Mother

This poem, out of chronological order here for contrast with the preceding poem, is the only surviving mention by Anne Bradstreet of her mother.

Upon the burning of our house

The title is from the Rev. Simon Bradstreet's notation in the small manuscript book (see Introduction and note to " To my Dear Children"):

    Here followes some verses upon the burning of our house,
  July 10th, 1666. Copyed out of a loose Paper.

    5. fire: "*Fire!*"

  37. chide,: (*read "chide:"*).

  47. It's] 'Its *E*

  54. lyes: *lie.*

Upon some distemper of body

    4. head,] head. *E*

  12. Main.] Main; *E*

In memory of . . . Elizabeth Bradstreet

    1. babe: *The child Elizabeth, the child Anne (see below), and the infant Simon were all children of Anne Bradstreet's eldest son*

Samuel, whose wife's death at 28 is also commemorated in a poem.   hearts: *heart's*   content: (*a noun here*).

6. thy *errata sheet*] the E

In memory of . . . Anne Bradstreet

7. below,] below? E
8. woe?] woe. E
9. flour: *flower.*

On my dear Grand-child Simon Bradstreet

Signed " A.B." in Ellis. This poem is perhaps the most poignant example of the author's grief struggling with Puritan dogma.

To the memory of . . . Mercy Bradstreet

Mercy Bradstreet, wife of Samuel Bradstreet (see note for " In Memory of my dear grand-child Elizabeth Bradstreet," above), died soon after the premature birth of a child. The poem is signed " A.B." in Ellis, who suggests that 1669 in the title is a misprint for 1670.

5. lopt the Tree: *lopped, the tree*
21. before, she: *before she*
27. She one hath left: *a daughter, Mercy, born November 20, 1667.*

To my Dear Children

Signed " A.B." in Ellis. All poems in this section (Section III) are included in the small manuscript book now in the possession of the Stevens Memorial Library at North Andover, Massachusetts. To his mother's handwritten prose " Meditations Divine and morall " (see Appendix B), which occupy the first 41 pages of the 98-page book, Simon Bradstreet added, in his own handwriting, the contents of a second manuscript book kept by Mrs. Bradstreet for her children and found among her papers at her death. It is from this second book, now lost, that these religious meditations come. All are in Simon's handwriting; of the poems in the extant manuscript book only " As weary pilgrim, now at rest" is in Mrs. Bradstreet's own handwriting (*see pages 38 and 39*). For more formal religious statements, see Section V, *Dialogues and Lamentations,* and *Appendix A.*

"*By night when others soundly slept*"

    10. teares: *see Psalm 56:8.*

For Deliverance from a feaver

    16. Mercyes Rowl: *The Bay Psalm Book translates "He trusted on the Lord" (Psalm 22:8) as "Upon the Lord he rold himself." (Ellis)*

From another sore Fitt

    10. loines: *see Proverbs 31:17.*

"*As spring the winter doth succeed*"

Dated May 13, 1657, in Ellis.

    5. Suns: *Sun's.*
    9. winters: *winter's.*
    20. Baca: *see Psalm 84:5–6.*
    21. I studious *E*] O studious *Hensley*

Samuel his goeing for England

Samuel Bradstreet, Mrs. Bradstreet's eldest son, graduated from Harvard in 1653. He sailed for England in November, 1657, and returned safely in July, 1661 (see below, "On my Sons Return . . .").

    4. many yeares: "It pleased God to keep me a long time without a child, which was a great greif to me."—*Anne Bradstreet's description of the early years of her marriage in her manuscript book.*
    16. thee] the *E*

"*My thankfull heart with glorying Tongue*"

    3. recur'd *E*] recured *Hensley*
    13. faitefull: *faithful.*

For the restoration of my dear Husband

    4. comforts: *see Psalm 71:21.*

Upon my Daughter Hannah Wiggin

Hannah married Andrew Wiggin, June 14, 1659, and died in 1707.

On my Sons Return out of England

See note for "Upon my Son Samuel his goeing for England," above. The manuscript poem ends with the note:

    O Lord, graunt that I may never forgett thy Loving kindnes in this Particular, and how gratiously thou hast answered my Desires.

    8. The other: *the ship of James Garrett was lost in passage in 1657.*
  19. royall ones: *Henry, Duke of Gloucester, and Mary, his sister, died of smallpox in 1660.*
  21. Incūbers: *Norton suggests "encumbers."*
  22. (Without all fraud)] Without (all fraud) *E*
  25. Eagles: *Eagles'.*   hether: *hither.*   brought: *see Exodus 19:4.*

Upon my . . . husband his goeing into England

In 1662, after the restoration of Charles II to the throne, Simon Bradstreet went to England with the Rev. John Norton to divert any possible anger that Charles might have toward the Colonists and to secure an extension of royal favor for the Massachusetts Bay Colony. On September 3 (see below, "In thankfull Remembrance . . .") they returned bearing a letter from the king confirming the charter privileges and pardoning past errors. See also the poems in Section I.

In my dear husband his Absence

See note to "Upon my dear and loving husband his goeing . . .," above.

    8. Thro' thee] Thro: the *E*
  21. do'st: *dost.*

27. thro'] thro: *E*
34. ha'st: *hast.*

Letters ... from my husband out of England

See note to "Upon my dear and loving husband his goeing ...," above.

    5, 6. heart, desert: (*probably a perfect rhyme then*).

My dear husbands safe Arrivall

Gov. Simon Bradstreet returned safely to New England in September, 1662. See note to "Upon my dear and loving husband his goeing ...," above. The manuscript poem is followed by a note in young Simon's handwriting: "This was the last Thing written in that Book by my dear and hon'd Mother."

    7. seases: *seizes.*

"As weary pilgrim, now at rest"

Dated "Aug: 31, 69" in Ellis, with the note that the original punctuation and spelling have been carefully followed. See pages 38 and 39 for facsimile of Mrs. Bradstreet's manuscript copy, the only poem extant in her handwriting.

    4. myrie: *miry.*
    15. gaule: *gall.*
    18. safity: *safety.*
    20, 30. with] wth *E*

Contemplations

    4. Where: *were.*
    8. wist: *to know.*
    14. here no: *here, no.*
    23. was: *were.*
    26. Universes: *Universe's.*
    34. heat *errata leaf*] heart *E*
    45, 46. high? ... mould: (*read as though question mark followed "mould"*).

51. lead: *led.*

53. mazed: *dazed, bewildered.*

67. moneths: *months.*

85. sacrifice] sacrfiice *E*

91. raise.] raise *E*

105. wals: *walls.*

124, 125. If winter come . . . A Spring: *These lines have been frequently pointed out as precursors of Shelley's famous line.*

127. stanza 19: *erroneously numbered 20 in second edition.*

130. obliterate: *(an adjective).*

135. longer: *(read as though followed by question mark).*

154. pace.] pace *E*

169. tast: *taste.*

183. stanza 27: *erroneously numbered 28 in second edition.*

185. cruciating: *tormenting.*

189. Reminds: *recall to mind.* fear.] fear *E*

190. prevent: *anticipate. "I prevented the dawning of the morning, and cried: I hoped in thy word." Psalm 119:145. See also I Thessalonians 4:15.*

196. legion.] legion *E*

203. Relation.] Relation *E*

219. sowre: *sour.*

231. white stone: *see Revelation 2:17.*

The Flesh and the Spirit

Samuel Eliot Morison suggests this is a dramatization of Romans 8; Josephine Piercy traces its source to such medieval debate literature as "The Owl and the Nightingale."

2. Lacrim: *from "lacrima" (Latin), a tear.*

43. ye: *yea.*

47. arise: *(a noun here).*

49. speak'st, hat'st] speak st, hat st *E*

66. off: *of.*

85. City: *see Revelation 21:10–27; 22:1–5.*

The Vanity of all worldly things

21. learning arts *E*] learning, arts *Hensley*

29. Stocks such: *Stocks, such.* Stoicks, Stocks: *a delightful Bradstreet pun. Thomas Thorpe in dedicating Healey's "Epictetus*

his Manuall" in *1610 wrote:* "He is more senceless than a
stocke that hath no good sence of this stoick."

34. Summum Bonum: *the highest good in Aristotelian ethics.*
38. account.] account *E*
56. And all the rest . . . find: *in first edition:*

> The rest's but vanity, and vain we find.

Davids Lamentation for Saul and Jonathan

*A verse paraphrase of 2 Samuel 1 : 19–27. Cf. "Tenth Muse" version
quoted in Piercy, "Anne Bradstreet."*

5. this thing *T*] this things *E*
17. crimson, blood] crimson blood *T*
33. wast] wert *T*
36. surpassing man] passing a man *T*
38–40. *The punctuation for the last three lines follows T rather
than E:* mine, . . . decay? . . . away?

A Dialogue between Old England and New . . . 1642

*Written in 1642 and published in 1650, this poem reflects the author's
love for England and her concern over the impending civil war. The
revisions date, in all likelihood, from about 1666.*

7. mournful] mourning *T*
26. wound's *T*] wound *E.* know *E*] know? *T*
36. Maud: *The Empress Matilda (1102–1167), daughter of
Henry I of England.* Stephen: *Son of Stephen of Blois,
Count Palatine of Champagne, and nephew of Henry I.*
44. Tushes: *tusks.* Boar: *Richard III, so called in Shakespeare.*
46. you] not *T*
58. maime: *maimed state.*
61. Alcies Son . . . Henryes daughter: *see note to line 36 above.
Stephen's mother was Adela, fourth daughter of William
the Conqueror; her name is sometimes given as Alice, here
contracted to Alcie.*
64. Lewis] Jews *E, a misprint for the Lewis of the first edition.*
69–70. No crafty Tyrant . . . great: *in first edition:*

No Crook-backt Tyrant, now usurps the Seat,
Whose tearing tusks did wound, and kill, and threat:

95. were] are *T*
111. by great ones done] which I have done *T*
112. Oh *errata leaf*] Of *E.* youths *E*] Babes *T*
115. For bribery Adultery and lyes] For Bribery, Adultery, for Thefts, and Lyes *T*
116. parallize: *find a parallel for.*
141. Rochel: *La Rochelle.*
170. Laud: *Archbishop Laud was confined in the Tower of London at the time of Mrs. Bradstreet's punning jest, and was not executed until January, 1645.*
197. inn: (*a verb here*).
202–203. For my relief . . . recompence that good . . . thee: *in first edition:*

> For my relief now use thy utmost skill,
> And recompence me good, for all my ill.

206. and I your flesh] I once your flesh *T*
218. who did] which do *T*
222. Mero: *Meroz* (*see Judges 5:23*).
227. Popelings] Prelates *T*
259. nourish;] nourish *E*
285. horses bells: *see Zechariah 14:20, 21.*
288. rightest cause] Parliament *T*

In Honour of . . . Queen Elizabeth

Dated 1643 in T, where "of happy memory" in the title reads "of most happy memory."

15. yerst: *formerly.*
20. Speeds, Cambdens: *John Speed and William Camden, who wrote histories of England in 1623 and 1635, respectively.*
24. 'leven] nine *T*
33. Salique law: *rule of succession forbidding females to succeed to certain titles.*
38. once] twice *T*
65. to: *too.*

This poem was considerably tightened and revised in the second edition. Only the most important revisions are included here; for a more detailed comparison, see Ellis, where both versions are complete.

9. Polimina: *Hensley has Polymnia (muse of the solemn hymn).*

18. one Volume: *from this Buchanan Charles deduces that Mrs. Bradstreet was familiar only with one or more of the successive one-volume editions of Sidney's collected works, but not with any of the manuscript copies or separate printings of individual works.*

24. men of morose minds envy his glory] modest Maids, and Wives, blush at thy glory *T*

33–36. *Omitted from second edition:*

> Yet great *Augustus* was content (we know)
> To be saluted by a silly Crow;
> Then let such Crowes as I, thy praises sing,
> A Crow's a Crow, and *Caesar* is a King.

36. ought: *owed.*

38. Whilst English blood yet runs within my veins: *in first edition:*

> Which have the self-same blood yet in my veines.

Ellis argues from the use of "self-same" and change to "English" that Anne Bradstreet believed she had a blood relationship to Sidney but that she later retracted the claim. Buchanan Charles points out that she may have made the change to avoid this very misinterpretation. Many efforts have been made to find a connection between her father, Thomas Dudley, and the family of Sidney's mother, Lady Mary Dudley, but so far all efforts, as Buchanan Charles points out, have been in vain.

62. sable: *cloak of mourning.*

69. Silvester: *Josuah Sylvester, who wrote "An Elegiac Epistle on the decease of Sir William Sidney."*

82. Errata . . . pen] Errata, through their leave threw me my pen *T. It has been suggested that the muse of lyric poetry, Erato, is meant.*

See *Introduction* for an account of du Bartas's influence on *Anne Bradstreet*.

24. Ladies tires: *Ladies' attires.*
52. Bartas: *Bartas's*
66. tongues.] tongues *E*
82. Song,] Song. *E*

The Tenth Muse (*title page*)

The Tenth Muse was published in London in 1650. The appearance of a book by a woman, and especially an American woman, called for some explaining, as in the following Note to the Reader (by her brother-in-law, the Rev. John Woodbridge), and lively lines from Nathaniel Ward.

Kind Reader:

Had I opportunity but to borrow some of the Authors wit, 'tis possible I might so trim this curious work with such quaint expressions, as that the Preface might bespeak thy further Perusal; but I fear 'twill be a shame for a Man that can speak so little, To be seen in the title-page of this Womans Book, lest by comparing the one with the other, the Reader should pass his sentence that it is the gift of women not only to speak most but to speak best; I shal leave therefore to commend that, which with any ingenious Reader will too much commend the Author, unless men turn more peevish than women, to envy the excellency of the inferiour Sex. I doubt not but the Reader will quickly find more than I can say, and the worst effect of his reading will be unbelief, which will make him question whether it be a womans work, and aske, Is it possible? If any do, take this as an answer from him that dares avow it; It is the Work of a Woman, honoured, and esteemed where she lives, for her gracious demeanour, her eminent parts, her pious conversation, her courteous disposition, her exact diligence in her place, and discreet managing of her Family occasions, and more than so, these Poems are the fruit but of some few houres, curtailed from her sleep and other refreshments. I dare adde little lest I keep thee too long; if thou wilt not believe the worth of these things (in their kind) when a man sayes it, yet believe it from a woman when thou seest it. This only I shall annex, I fear the displeasure of no person in the publishing of these Poems but the Author, without whose knowledg, and contrary to her expectation, I have presumed to bring to publick view, what she resolved in such a manner should never see the Sun; but I found that diverse had gotten some scattered Papers, affected them well, were likely to have sent forth broken pieces, to the Authors prejudice, which I thought to prevent, as well as to pleasure those that earnestly desired the view of the whole.

* *

Mercury shew'd Apollo, Bartas Book,
Minerva this, and wisht him well to look,
And tell uprightly which did which excell,
He view'd and view'd, and vow'd he could not tel.
They bid him Hemisphear his mouldy nose,
With's crackt leering glasses, for it would pose
The best brains he had in's old pudding-pan,
Sex weigh'd, which best, the Woman, or the Man?
He peer'd and por'd, & glar'd, & said for wore,
I'me even as wise now, as I was before:
They both 'gan laugh, and said it was no mar'l
The Auth'ress was a right Du Bartas Girle.
Good sooth quoth the old Don, tell ye me so,
I muse whither at length these Girls will go;
It half revives my chil frost-bitten blood,
To see a Woman once, do ought that's good;
And chode by Chaucers Boots, and Homers Furrs,
Let Men look to't, least Women wear the Spurrs.
                                        N. Ward.

Eight other laudatory poems preceded The Tenth Muse itself, and may be found in Ellis.

To her most Honoured Father Thomas Dudley . . .

This dedication prefacing the author's four quaternions in "The Tenth Muse" is signed "Anne Bradstreet" and dated March 20, 1642 in Ellis. The original marginal note to the phrase "your four

*Sisters" (line 2)—"T.D. On the four parts of the world"—apparently
refers to a now unknown poem by her father.*

    2. cloth'd] deckt *T*
  10. four, *T*] four *E*
  11. my four times four] my four; and four *T*
  16. attend. *T*] attend *E*
  17. have, *T*] have *E*
  24. rimes. *T*] rimes *E*
  27. foures] four *T*
  34. friend, *T*] friend *E*
  44. boundlesse *T*] boundess *E*

The Prologue

The initials "A.B." are appended in the first edition.

  19. Greek: *Demosthenes.*
  20. in future times speak plain] speake afterwards more plaine
      T
  22. his striving paine: *T*] his, striving pain *E*
  46. Give Thyme or] Give wholsome *T*
  47. ure: *ore.*
  48. your glistering gold but *T*] you glistring gold, but *E*

The Four Elements

  16. force, *T*] force *E*
  24. The noblest and most active Element.] Being the most
      impatient Element. *T*
  40. barr'd. *T*] bar'd *E*
  71. beasts *T*] beast *E*
  79–84. Crab . . . Boys: *names of constellations.* Bernice Hare:
      the constellation Berenice's Hair, or Coma Berenices.
  102. second Pliny: *Ellis suggests that the poet does not mean the
      younger Pliny, but translates the cognomen of "Secundus,"
      which belonged to both Plinys.*
  116–118. My raging flame . . . risen New: *This reference to the
      Great Fire of London of 1666 was added in the revisions
      for the second edition.*
  120. So *errata leaf*] Lo *E*

134. fire: *T*] fire *E*

152. hundreds: (*probably pronounced with three syllables at that time*).

171. leap] skip *T*

228. The Mother on her tender infant flyes] The tender mother on her Infant flyes; *T*

242. Dathan] Korah *T. See Numbers 16.*

243. Roman: *Marcus Curtius, who allegedly rode into a chasm in the Forum to close it.*

275. chops *E*] chaps *errata leaf*

329–330. And be . . . deep: *in first edition:*

> But note this maxime in Philosophy:
> Then Seas are deep, Mountains are never high.

342. list: *please.*

350. ill] force *T*

359. Grasier do] Plowman both *T*

372. mighty country: *Atlantis.*

386. Noe: *Noah.*

392. *Air.*] *Air, E*

408. least: *lest.*

441. Sages either] Sages did, or *T*

444. Earths . . . waters: *Earth's . . . water's.*

458. flown, *T*] flown *E*

466. Millain: *Milan.*

482. worth *errata leaf, T*] wrath *E*

Of the four Humours in Mans Constitution

69. musing she sits *errata leaf, T*] musing sits *E*

107. Alas] No, no *T*

118. thy *errata leaf*] the *E*

126. adustion: *burning, state of being burnt.*

131. Both *errata leaf*] But *E*] Thus *T*

136. friend and foe *errata leaf, T*] it, foe, friend, *E*

145. nor *E*] not *T*

146. Do's . . . flat: *first edition follows with:*

> The spongy Lungs, I feed with frothy blood.
> They coole my heat, and so repay my good.

153. sparing *T*] sparings *E*

176. lies. *T*] lies *E*
186. Hilt] Hill *E*
220. diabolical *T*] diabolibal *E*
237. natural] th' natural *T*
243. the] thee *T*
268. There *T*] Their *E*
282. intends: *T*] intends *E*
283. shent: *reproached.*
309. seizes] ceases *T*
348. bitternesse *T*] bittererss *E*
361. girds: *gibes.*
362. venter: *venture.*
385. more: *T*] more *E*
481. see. *T*] see *E*
507. grace; *T*] grace *E*
511. Knights: (*read as though followed by a comma*).
518. thee *T*] the *E*
568. Crooke: *Helkiah Crooke, author of "Description of the Body of Man" (1615, 1618, 1634).*
596. melancholy] Melanchollies *T*
603. here's *errata leaf, T*] here *E*
605. Flegme *T*] flegm *E*

Of the four Ages of Man

This poem is particularly interesting because the revisions date from about 1666, six years after the restoration of Charles II, and reflect, therefore, the changing political climate in New England. In such lines as 405–406 ("What are my thoughts, this is no time to say. / Men may more freely speak another day"), one finds an attitude of quiet caution. Miss Piercy points out that there is less contention and more actual observation in this quaternion than in the other three.

1. act] acts *T*
58. than's] then's *E*
89. cark: *worry.*
92. presence] presents *T*
98. King] Prince *T*
138. preserv'd *T*] presev'd *E*

198. pounce: *sprinkle with powder.*

216. affrights] affrighrs *E*

217–218. Sometimes . . . scarrs: *in first edition:*

> Sometimes the loathsome Pox, my face be-mars,
> With ugly marks of his eternal scars;

225–226. *The first edition has*

> Of Marrow ful my bones, of Milk my breasts,
> Ceas'd by the gripes of Serjeant Death's arrests:

Cf. the dying Hamlet (V, 2, 350–351):

> . . . as this fell sergeant, death,
> Is strict in his arrest . . .

Piercy shows other instances of Anne Bradstreet's familiarity with Shakespeare despite Puritan disapproval of him.

228. yea] ye *E*

238. Such *errata leaf, T*] My *E*

280. My wakeful . . . gain: *first edition follows with:*

> For restlesse day and night, I'm rob'd of sleep,
> By cankered care, who centinel doth keep.

314. I . . . within: "*Omnia mea mecum porto*" (*I carry all my possessions with me*). Bias: *One of the Seven Wise Men of Ancient Greece, quoted in Cicero's "Paradoxa Stoicorum," I, 1, 8.*

336. Bis pueri senes: "*Old men are children twice over.*"

358. she: *Queen Elizabeth.*

361. Cales: *former English name of the city of Cadiz, in Spain. The shipping in its harbor was burned by Sir Francis Drake in 1587, and the city was sacked by the Earl of Essex and Lord Charles Howard in 1596.*

369–405. *These lines are considerably revised from the 1650 version. See Ellis for a comparison of the two editions.*

369. king: *James I.*

371. Prince: *Henry, Prince of Wales, died November 6, 1612, at the age of 19.*

380. royal one: *The Elector Palatine Frederick V.*

383. Ree: *The Isle of Rhé.* Rochel: *La Rochelle.* Rochel] Cades *T*

389. one stab'd: *Buckingham.* some: *Charles I, Archbishop Laud, the Earl of Strafford, among others.*

395. slaughtered: *in the insurrection in Ireland in 1641.*

399. King: *Charles I.*

400. Usurper: *Cromwell.*

402. ye *E.* Hensley has "yet," following *T and some copies of the 1678 edition.*

405–406. *Miss Piercy asks in regard to these two lines, "Is it monarchy she fears or is it local Puritan opinion?"*

425. golden Bowl, silver Cord: *in Ecclesiastes 12:6, symbols of long life.*

435. pleasant'st *T*] pleasants *E*

The four Seasons of the Year

44. thence; *T*] thence *E*

58. gleads: *gledes, birds of prey.* gleads. *T*] gleads *E*

67. witty] buzzing *T*

84. decline. *T*] decline: *E*

89. off] of *E*

103. shepheard lad, *T*] Shepherd Lads *E*

113. Bajazet: *Bajazet I, 1347–1403, Ottoman sultan defeated by Tamerlane in 1402. Cf. Marlowe's "Tamburlaine the Great."*

114. lose] lose. *T, E*

115. Orthobulus: *son of Bajazet I.*

124. surpasses; *T*] surpasses *E*

139. prize,] prize. *E*

150. Manchet: *loaf or roll of fine wheat bread.*

158. Rock. *T*] Rock *E*

190. scited: *cited.*

211. Groanland] Groen-land *T*

240. leese: *lose.*

258. *Signed in the first edition:* Your dutifull Daughter./ A.B.

The four Monarchyes

Of this long poem, largely a poetic retelling of Sir Walter Ralegh's "History of the World," only a single incident is here reproduced. For the entire poem, see Ellis (Peter Smith, Gloucester, Mass.), pp. 181–329.

6. Cush *T*] Chus *E*

64. Mene, Tekel: *see Daniel 5:25–28.*
71. "An Apology": *for not completing "The four Monarchyes," abandoned after the burning of her home.*
75. large,] large *E*
84. fire: *see the poem "Upon the burning of our house, July 10th, 1666," page 54.*

Appendix B: Meditations Divine and morall (selections)

The indented numbers refer to the lines of prose text.

Meditation 4

1. ship *BC*] SHIP *E*
2. overset, *BC*] overset; *E*

Meditation 17

2 (*seventh word*). what *BC*] What *E*
3. *The mark after "received" is exactly as in the manuscript (BC).*

Meditation 26

2. *Manuscript is smudged after "Commonwealth" (BC).*

Meditation 45

2, 3. marble hearted *BC*] marble-hearted *E*
3. contrition, *BC*] contrition; *E*

Meditation 53

6. comforts *BC*] comforts; *E*

SELECTED BIBLIOGRAPHY

Editions of Anne Bradstreet's Works

Bradstreet, Anne. *The Tenth Muse Lately sprung up in America. Or Severall Poems, compiled with great variety of Wit and Learning, full of delight. Wherein especially is contained a compleat discourse and description of The Four Elements, Constitutions, Ages of Man, Seasons of the Year. Together with an Exact Epitomie of the Four Monarchies, viz. The Assyrian, Persian, Grecian, Roman. Also a Dialogue between Old England and New, concerning the late troubles. With divers other pleasant and serious Poems.* By a Gentlewoman in those parts. Printed at London for Stephen Bowtell at the signe of the Bible in Popes Head-Alley, 1650.

————. *Several Poems Compiled with great variety of Wit and Learning, full of Delight; Wherein especially is contained a compleat Discourse, and Description of The Four Elements. Constitutions, Ages of Man, Seasons of the Year. Together with an exact Epitome of the three first Monarchyes Viz. The Assyrian, Persian, Grecian. And beginning of the Romane Common-wealth to the end of their last King: With diverse other pleasant & serious Poems,* By a Gentlewoman in New-England. The second Edition, Corrected by the Author, and enlarged by an Addition of several other Poems found amongst her Papers after her Death. Boston, Printed by John Foster, 1678.

————. *Several Poems. . . .* The Third Edition . . . Re-printed from the second Edition, in the Year M.DCC.LVIII. [Boston.]

————. *The Works of Anne Bradstreet in Prose and Verse.* Edited by John Harvard Ellis. Printed in Cambridge for Abram E. Cutter of Charlestown, 1867. [Reprinted by Peter Smith, Gloucester, Mass., in 1932 and 1962.]

Norton, Charles Eliot, ed. *The Poems of Mrs. Anne Bradstreet, Together with Her Prose Remains.* The Duodecimos, MDCCCXCVII.

Piercy, Josephine K., ed. *The Tenth Muse (1650) and, from the manuscripts, Meditations Divine and Morall together with Letters and Occasional Pieces by Anne Bradstreet.* Facsimile reproductions. Gainesville, Florida: Scholars' Facsimiles & Reprints, 1965.

Hensley, Jeannine, ed. *The Works of Anne Bradstreet.* Foreword by Adrienne Rich. Cambridge, Mass.: The John Harvard Library, The Belknap Press of Harvard University Press, 1967.

Works about Anne Bradstreet and Her Times

Berryman, John. *Homage to Mistress Bradstreet.* New York: Farrar, Straus and Cudahy, 1956. [Reprinted in *Homage to Mistress Bradstreet and Other Poems.* New York: Noonday Press, 1968.]

Caldwell, Col. Luther. *An Account of Anne Bradstreet, the Puritan Poetess and Kindred Topics.* Boston: Damrell & Upham, 1898.

Campbell, Helen. *Anne Bradstreet and Her Time.* Boston: D. Lothrop Co., 1891.

Charles, Buchanan. "Anne Bradstreet Manuscript Acquired by North Andover Library," *The Bay State Librarian*, Winter (January), 1956.

Griswold, Rufus Wilmot. *The Female Poets of America.* Philadelphia, Carey and Hart, 1848.

Jantz, Harold S. *The First Century of New England Verse.* New York: Russell and Russell, 1962.

Miller, Perry, ed. *The American Puritans: Their Prose and Poetry.* New York: Doubleday Anchor Books, 1956.

Morison, Samuel Eliot. *Intellectual Life of Colonial New England.* Ithaca, N.Y.: Cornell University Great Seal Books, 1960. [Reprint of second edition of *The Puritan Pronaos*, 1936, 1956.]

Piercy, Josephine K. *Anne Bradstreet.* New Haven, Conn.: College & University Press (in Twayne's United States Authors Series), 1965.

Powell, Sumner Chilton. *Puritan Village: The Formation of a New England Town.* Middletown, Conn.: Wesleyan University Press, 1963.

Stanford, Ann. "Anne Bradstreet: Dogmatist and Rebel," *The New England Quarterly*, September, 1966.

Tyler, Moses Coit. *A History of American Literature, 1607–1765*. New York: G. P. Putnam's Sons, 1897.

Wertenbaker, Thomas Jefferson. *The Puritan Oligarchy: The Founding of American Civilization*. New York: Charles Scribner's Sons, 1947.

Whicher, George F., ed. *Alas, All's Vanity*. . . . New York: Spiral Press for Collectors' Bookshop, 1942.

White, Elizabeth Wade. "The Tenth Muse—A Tercentenary Appraisal of Anne Bradstreet," *The William and Mary Quarterly*, VIII, No. 3 (July, 1951).

INDEX OF TITLES AND FIRST LINES

Poem titles are in italic, first lines in Roman type

A Worthy Matron of unspotted life   54

Alas dear Mother, fairest Queen and best   95

Alas slain is the Head of Israel   94

All Praise to him who hath now turn'd   70

All things within this fading world hath end   45

Although great Queen thou now in silence lye   105

Among the happy wits this age hath shown   112

And live I still to see Relations gone   58

Another four I've left yet to bring on   167

As he said vanity, so vain say I   92

As loving Hind that (Hartless) wants her Deer   41

As spring the winter doth succeed   67

As weary pilgrim, now at rest   77

Author to her Book, The   40

Before the Birth of one of her Children   45

Bles't bee thy Name, who did'st restore   70

By duty bound, and not by custome led   51

By night when others soundly slept   61

Contemplations   79

Davids Lamentation for Saul and Jonathan   94

Dear Sir of late delighted with the sight   117

Deliverance from a fitt of Fainting   64

Dialogue between Old England and New; concerning their present Troubles, Anno, 1642, A   95

Du Bartas, In honour of   112

Elegie upon that Honourable and renowned Knight Sir Philip Sidney, who was untimely slain at the Siege of Zutphen, Anno, 1586   109

Elizabeth, Queen [Elegy on]   105

Epitaph On my dear and ever honoured Mother Mrs. Dorothy Dudley, who deceased Decemb. 27. 1643. and of her age, 61, An   54

Farewel dear babe, my hearts too much content   57

Flesh and the Spirit, The   89

For Deliverance from a feaver   62

For the restoration of my dear Husband from a burning Ague, June,
1661   69

Four Ages of Man, Of the   153

Four Elements, The   120

Four Humours in Mans Constitution, Of the   135

Four Monarchyes, the Assyrian being the first, beginning under
Nimrod, 131. Years after the Flood, The   175

Four Seasons of the Year, The   167

From another sore Fitt   63

I had eight birds hatcht in one nest   47

If ever two were one, then surely we   41

In anguish of my heart repleat with woes   56

In honour of Du Bartas, 1641   112

In Honour of that High and Mighty Princess Queen Elizabeth of
happy memory   105

In memory of my dear grand-child Anne Bradstreet. Who deceased
June 20. 1669. being three years and seven Moneths old   57

In memory of my dear grand-child Elizabeth Bradstreet, who
deceased August, 1665. being a year and a half old   57

In my distresse I sought the Lord   63

In my Solitary houres in my dear husband his Absence   74

In reference to her Children, 23. June, 1656   47

In secret place where once I stood   89

In silent night when rest I took   54

In thankfull acknowledgment for the letters I received from my
husband out of England   76

In thankfull Remembrance for my dear husbands safe Arrivall
Sept. 3, 1662   76

Letter to her Husband, absent upon Publick employment, A   44

Lo now four other act upon the stage   153

Most truly honoured, and as truly dear   51

My head, my heart, mine Eyes, my life, nay more   44

My soul, rejoice thou in thy God   66

My thankfull heart with glorying Tongue   68

No sooner come, but gone, and fal'n asleep   58

O Lord, thou hear'st my dayly moan   74
O Thou most high who rulest All   72
O Thou that hear'st the Prayers of Thine   76
Of the four Ages of Man   153
Of the four Humours in Mans Constitution   135
On my dear Grand-child Simon Bradstreet, Who dyed on 16.
  Novemb. 1669. being but a moneth, and one day old   58
On my Sons Return out of England, July 17, 1661   70

Phœbus make haste, the day's too long, be gone   42
Prologue, The [to The Tenth Muse]   118

Sidney, Sir Philip [Elegy on]   109
Some time now past in the Autumnal Tide   79

The Fire, Air, Earth and water did contest   120
The former four now ending their discourse   135
This Book by Any yet unread   61
Thou ill-form'd offspring of my feeble brain   40
Thou mighty God of Sea and Land   68
To her Father with some verses   51
To her most Honoured Father Thomas Dudley Esq; these humbly
  presented   117
To my Dear and loving Husband   41
To my Dear Children   61
To sing of Wars, of Captains, and of Kings   118
To the Memory of my dear and ever honoured Father Thomas
  Dudley Esq; Who deceased, July 31. 1653. and of his Age, 77   51
To the memory of my dear Daughter in Law, Mrs. Mercy Bradstreet,
  who deceased Sept. 6. 1669. in the 28. year of her Age   58
Twice ten years old, not fully told   50

Upon a Fit of Sickness, Anno. 1632. Ætatis suæ, 19   50
Upon my Daughter Hannah Wiggin her recovery from a dangerous
  feaver   70
Upon my dear and loving husband his goeing into England, Jan. 16,
  1661   72
Upon my Son Samuel his goeing for England, Novem. 6, 1657   68

Upon some distemper of body   56
Upon the burning of our house, July 10th, 1666   54

Vanity of all worldly things, The   92

What God is like to him I serve   65
What shall I render to thy Name   76
When England did enjoy her Halsion dayes   109
When feares and sorrowes me besett   69
When Sorrowes had begyrt me round   62
When time was young, and World in Infancy   175
With troubled heart and trembling hand I write   57
Worthy art Thou, O Lord of praise   64

A CATALOGUE OF SELECTED DOVER BOOKS
IN ALL FIELDS OF INTEREST

A CATALOGUE OF SELECTED DOVER BOOKS
IN ALL FIELDS OF INTEREST

WHAT IS SCIENCE?, *N. Campbell*
The role of experiment and measurement, the function of mathematics, the nature of scientific laws, the difference between laws and theories, the limitations of science, and many similarly provocative topics are treated clearly and without technicalities by an eminent scientist. "Still an excellent introduction to scientific philosophy," H. Margenau in *Physics Today*. "A first-rate primer . . . deserves a wide audience," *Scientific American*. 192pp. 5⅜ x 8.
S43   Paperbound $1.25

THE NATURE OF LIGHT AND COLOUR IN THE OPEN AIR, *M. Minnaert*
Why are shadows sometimes blue, sometimes green, or other colors depending on the light and surroundings? What causes mirages? Why do multiple suns and moons appear in the sky? Professor Minnaert explains these unusual phenomena and hundreds of others in simple, easy-to-understand terms based on optical laws and the properties of light and color. No mathematics is required but artists, scientists, students, and everyone fascinated by these "tricks" of nature will find thousands of useful and amazing pieces of information. Hundreds of observational experiments are suggested which require no special equipment. 200 illustrations; 42 photos. xvi + 362pp. 5⅜ x 8.
T196   Paperbound $2.00

THE STRANGE STORY OF THE QUANTUM, AN ACCOUNT FOR THE GENERAL READER OF THE GROWTH OF IDEAS UNDERLYING OUR PRESENT ATOMIC KNOWLEDGE, *B. Hoffmann*
Presents lucidly and expertly, with barest amount of mathematics, the problems and theories which led to modern quantum physics. Dr. Hoffmann begins with the closing years of the 19th century, when certain trifling discrepancies were noticed, and with illuminating analogies and examples takes you through the brilliant concepts of Planck, Einstein, Pauli, Broglie, Bohr, Schroedinger, Heisenberg, Dirac, Sommerfeld, Feynman, etc. This edition includes a new, long postscript carrying the story through 1958. "Of the books attempting an account of the history and contents of our modern atomic physics which have come to my attention, this is the best," H. Margenau, Yale University, in *American Journal of Physics*. 32 tables and line illustrations. Index. 275pp. 5⅜ x 8.
T518   Paperbound $2.00

GREAT IDEAS OF MODERN MATHEMATICS: THEIR NATURE AND USE, *Jagjit Singh*
Reader with only high school math will understand main mathematical ideas of modern physics, astronomy, genetics, psychology, evolution, etc. better than many who use them as tools, but comprehend little of their basic structure. Author uses his wide knowledge of non-mathematical fields in brilliant exposition of differential equations, matrices, group theory, logic, statistics, problems of mathematical foundations, imaginary numbers, vectors, etc. Original publication. 2 appendixes. 2 indexes. 65 ills. 322pp. 5⅜ x 8.
T587   Paperbound $2.00

A SHORT ACCOUNT OF THE HISTORY OF MATHEMATICS,
W. W. Rouse Ball
Last previous edition (1908) hailed by mathematicians and laymen for lucid overview of math as living science, for understandable presentation of individual contributions of great mathematicians. Treats lives, discoveries of every important school and figure from Egypt, Phoenicia to late nineteenth century. Greek schools of Ionia, Cyzicus, Alexandria, Byzantium, Pythagoras; primitive arithmetic; Middle Ages and Renaissance, including European and Asiatic contributions; modern math of Descartes, Pascal, Wallis, Huygens, Newton, Euler, Lambert, Laplace, scores more. More emphasis on historical development, exposition of ideas than other books on subject. Non-technical, readable text can be followed with no more preparation than high-school algebra. Index. 544pp. 5⅜ x 8. Paperbound $2.25

GREAT IDEAS AND THEORIES OF MODERN COSMOLOGY, *Jagjit Singh*
Companion volume to author's popular "Great Ideas of Modern Mathematics" (Dover, $2.00). The best non-technical survey of post-Einstein attempts to answer perhaps unanswerable questions of origin, age of Universe, possibility of life on other worlds, etc. Fundamental theories of cosmology and cosmogony recounted, explained, evaluated in light of most recent data: Einstein's concepts of relativity, space-time; Milne's a priori world-system; astrophysical theories of Jeans, Eddington; Hoyle's "continuous creation;" contributions of dozens more scientists. A faithful, comprehensive critical summary of complex material presented in an extremely well-written text intended for laymen. Original publication. Index. xii + 276pp. 5⅜ x 8½. Paperbound $2.00

THE RESTLESS UNIVERSE, *Max Born*
A remarkably lucid account by a Nobel Laureate of recent theories of wave mechanics, behavior of gases, electrons and ions, waves and particles, electronic structure of the atom, nuclear physics, and similar topics. "Much more thorough and deeper than most attempts . . . easy and delightful," *Chemical and Engineering News*. Special feature: 7 animated sequences of 60 figures each showing such phenomena as gas molecules in motion, the scattering of alpha particles, etc. 11 full-page plates of photographs. Total of nearly 600 illustrations. 351pp. 6⅛ x 9¼. Paperbound $2.00

PLANETS, STARS AND GALAXIES: DESCRIPTIVE ASTRONOMY FOR BEGINNERS,
A. E. Fanning
What causes the progression of the seasons? Phases of the moon? The Aurora Borealis? How much does the sun weigh? What are the chances of life on our sister planets? Absorbing introduction to astronomy, incorporating the latest discoveries and theories: the solar wind, the surface temperature of Venus, the pock-marked face of Mars, quasars, and much more. Places you on the frontiers of one of the most vital sciences of our time. Revised (1966). Introduction by Donald H. Menzel, Harvard University. References. Index. 45 illustrations. 189pp. 5¼ x 8¼. Paperbound $1.50

GREAT IDEAS IN INFORMATION THEORY, LANGUAGE AND CYBERNETICS,
Jagjit Singh
Non-mathematical, but profound study of information, language, the codes used by men and machines to communicate, the principles of analog and digital computers, work of McCulloch, Pitts, von Neumann, Turing, and Uttley, correspondences between intricate mechanical network of "thinking machines" and more intricate neurophysiological mechanism of human brain. Indexes. 118 figures. 50 tables. ix + 338pp. 5⅜ x 8½. Paperbound $2.00

THE MUSIC OF THE SPHERES: THE MATERIAL UNIVERSE — FROM ATOM TO QUASAR, SIMPLY EXPLAINED, *Guy Murchie*
Vast compendium of fact, modern concept and theory, observed and calculated data, historical background guides intelligent layman through the material universe. Brilliant exposition of earth's construction, explanations for moon's craters, atmospheric components of Venus and Mars (with data from recent fly-by's), sun spots, sequences of star birth and death, neighboring galaxies, contributions of Galileo, Tycho Brahe, Kepler, etc.; and (Vol. 2) construction of the atom (describing newly discovered sigma and xi subatomic particles), theories of sound, color and light, space and time, including relativity theory, quantum theory, wave theory, probability theory, work of Newton, Maxwell, Faraday, Einstein, de Broglie, etc. "Best presentation yet offered to the intelligent general reader," *Saturday Review*. Revised (1967). Index. 319 illustrations by the author. Total of xx + 644pp. 5⅜ x 8½.
Vol. 1 Paperbound $2.00, Vol. 2 Paperbound $2.00,
The set $4.00

FOUR LECTURES ON RELATIVITY AND SPACE, *Charles Proteus Steinmetz*
Lecture series, given by great mathematician and electrical engineer, generally considered one of the best popular-level expositions of special and general relativity theories and related questions. Steinmetz translates complex mathematical reasoning into language accessible to laymen through analogy, example and comparison. Among topics covered are relativity of motion, location, time; of mass; acceleration; 4-dimensional time-space; geometry of the gravitational field; curvature and bending of space; non-Euclidean geometry. Index. 40 illustrations. x + 142pp. 5⅜ x 8½.					Paperbound $1.35

HOW TO KNOW THE WILD FLOWERS, *Mrs. William Starr Dana*
Classic nature book that has introduced thousands to wonders of American wild flowers. Color-season principle of organization is easy to use, even by those with no botanical training, and the genial, refreshing discussions of history, folklore, uses of over 1,000 native and escape flowers, foliage plants are informative as well as fun to read. Over 170 full-page plates, collected from several editions, may be colored in to make permanent records of finds. Revised to conform with 1950 edition of Gray's Manual of Botany. xlii + 438pp. 5⅜ x 8½.					Paperbound $2.00

MANUAL OF THE TREES OF NORTH AMERICA, *Charles Sprague Sargent*
Still unsurpassed as most comprehensive, reliable study of North American tree characteristics, precise locations and distribution. By dean of American dendrologists. Every tree native to U.S., Canada, Alaska; 185 genera, 717 species, described in detail—leaves, flowers, fruit, winterbuds, bark, wood, growth habits, etc. plus discussion of varieties and local variants, immaturity variations. Over 100 keys, including unusual 11-page analytical key to genera, aid in identification. 783 clear illustrations of flowers, fruit, leaves. An unmatched permanent reference work for all nature lovers. Second enlarged (1926) edition. Synopsis of families. Analytical key to genera. Glossary of technical terms. Index. 783 illustrations, 1 map. Total of 982pp. 5⅜ x 8.
Vol. 1 Paperbound $2.25, Vol. 2 Paperbound $2.25,
The set $4.50

IT'S FUN TO MAKE THINGS FROM SCRAP MATERIALS,
Evelyn Glantz Hershoff
What use are empty spools, tin cans, bottle tops? What can be made from
rubber bands, clothes pins, paper clips, and buttons? This book provides
simply worded instructions and large diagrams showing you how to make
cookie cutters, toy trucks, paper turkeys, Halloween masks, telephone sets,
aprons, linoleum block- and spatter prints — in all 399 projects! Many are easy
enough for young children to figure out for themselves; some challenging
enough to entertain adults; all are remarkably ingenious ways to make things
from materials that cost pennies or less! Formerly "Scrap Fun for Everyone."
Index. 214 illustrations. 373pp. 5⅜ x 8½. Paperbound $1.50

SYMBOLIC LOGIC and THE GAME OF LOGIC, *Lewis Carroll*
"Symbolic Logic" is not concerned with modern symbolic logic, but is instead
a collection of over 380 problems posed with charm and imagination, using
the syllogism and a fascinating diagrammatic method of drawing conclusions.
In "The Game of Logic" Carroll's whimsical imagination devises a logical game
played with 2 diagrams and counters (included) to manipulate hundreds of
tricky syllogisms. The final section, "Hit or Miss" is a lagniappe of 101 addi-
tional puzzles in the delightful Carroll manner. Until this reprint edition,
both of these books were rarities costing up to $15 each. Symbolic Logic:
Index. xxxi + 199pp. The Game of Logic: 96pp. 2 vols. bound as one. 5⅜ x 8.
Paperbound $2.00

MATHEMATICAL PUZZLES OF SAM LOYD, PART I
selected and edited by M. Gardner
Choice puzzles by the greatest American puzzle creator and innovator. Selected
from his famous collection, "Cyclopedia of Puzzles," they retain the unique
style and historical flavor of the originals. There are posers based on arithmetic,
algebra, probability, game theory, route tracing, topology, counter and sliding
block, operations research, geometrical dissection. Includes the famous "14-15"
puzzle which was a national craze, and his "Horse of a Different Color" which
sold millions of copies. 117 of his most ingenious puzzles in all. 120 line
drawings and diagrams. Solutions. Selected references. xx + 167pp. 5⅜ x 8.
Paperbound $1.00

STRING FIGURES AND HOW TO MAKE THEM, *Caroline Furness Jayne*
107 string figures plus variations selected from the best primitive and modern
examples developed by Navajo, Apache, pygmies of Africa, Eskimo, in Europe,
Australia, China, etc. The most readily understandable, easy-to-follow book in
English on perennially popular recreation. Crystal-clear exposition; step-by-
step diagrams. Everyone from kindergarten children to adults looking for
unusual diversion will be endlessly amused. Index. Bibliography. Introduction
by A. C. Haddon. 17 full-page plates, 960 illustrations. xxiii + 401pp. 5⅜ x 8½.
Paperbound $2.00

PAPER FOLDING FOR BEGINNERS, *W. D. Murray and F. J. Rigney*
A delightful introduction to the varied and entertaining Japanese art of
origami (paper folding), with a full, crystal-clear text that anticipates every
difficulty; over 275 clearly labeled diagrams of all important stages in creation.
You get results at each stage, since complex figures are logically developed
from simpler ones. 43 different pieces are explained: sailboats, frogs, roosters,
etc. 6 photographic plates. 279 diagrams. 95pp. 5⅝ x 8⅜. Paperbound $1.00

PRINCIPLES OF ART HISTORY,
H. Wölfflin
Analyzing such terms as "baroque," "classic," "neoclassic," "primitive," "picturesque," and 164 different works by artists like Botticelli, van Cleve, Dürer, Hobbema, Holbein, Hals, Rembrandt, Titian, Brueghel, Vermeer, and many others, the author establishes the classifications of art history and style on a firm, concrete basis. This classic of art criticism shows what really occurred between the 14th-century primitives and the sophistication of the 18th century in terms of basic attitudes and philosophies. "A remarkable lesson in the art of seeing," *Sat. Rev. of Literature.* Translated from the 7th German edition. 150 illustrations. 254pp. 6⅛ x 9¼. Paperbound $2.00

PRIMITIVE ART,
Franz Boas
This authoritative and exhaustive work by a great American anthropologist covers the entire gamut of primitive art. Pottery, leatherwork, metal work, stone work, wood, basketry, are treated in detail. Theories of primitive art, historical depth in art history, technical virtuosity, unconscious levels of patterning, symbolism, styles, literature, music, dance, etc. A must book for the interested layman, the anthropologist, artist, handicrafter (hundreds of unusual motifs), and the historian. Over 900 illustrations (50 ceramic vessels, 12 totem poles, etc.). 376pp. 5⅜ x 8. Paperbound $2.25

THE GENTLEMAN AND CABINET MAKER'S DIRECTOR,
Thomas Chippendale
A reprint of the 1762 catalogue of furniture designs that went on to influence generations of English and Colonial and Early Republic American furniture makers. The 200 plates, most of them full-page sized, show Chippendale's designs for French (Louis XV), Gothic, and Chinese-manner chairs, sofas, canopy and dome beds, cornices, chamber organs, cabinets, shaving tables, commodes, picture frames, frets, candle stands, chimney pieces, decorations, etc. The drawings are all elegant and highly detailed; many include construction diagrams and elevations. A supplement of 24 photographs shows surviving pieces of original and Chippendale-style pieces of furniture. Brief biography of Chippendale by N. I. Bienenstock, editor of *Furniture World.* Reproduced from the 1762 edition. 200 plates, plus 19 photographic plates. vi + 249pp. 9⅛ x 12¼. Paperbound $3.50

AMERICAN ANTIQUE FURNITURE: A BOOK FOR AMATEURS,
Edgar G. Miller, Jr.
Standard introduction and practical guide to identification of valuable American antique furniture. 2115 illustrations, mostly photographs taken by the author in 148 private homes, are arranged in chronological order in extensive chapters on chairs, sofas, chests, desks, bedsteads, mirrors, tables, clocks, and other articles. Focus is on furniture accessible to the collector, including simpler pieces and a larger than usual coverage of Empire style. Introductory chapters identify structural elements, characteristics of various styles, how to avoid fakes, etc. "We are frequently asked to name some book on American furniture that will meet the requirements of the novice collector, the beginning dealer, and . . . the general public. . . . We believe Mr. Miller's two volumes more completely satisfy this specification than any other work," *Antiques.* Appendix. Index. Total of vi + 1106pp. 7⅞ x 10¾.

Two volume set, paperbound $7.50

THE BAD CHILD'S BOOK OF BEASTS, MORE BEASTS FOR WORSE CHILDREN, and A MORAL ALPHABET, *H. Belloc*
Hardly and anthology of humorous verse has appeared in the last 50 years without at least a couple of these famous nonsense verses. But one must see the entire volumes — with all the delightful original illustrations by Sir Basil Blackwood — to appreciate fully Belloc's charming and witty verses that play so subacidly on the platitudes of life and morals that beset his day — and ours. A great humor classic. Three books in one. Total of 157pp. 5⅜ x 8.
Paperbound $1.00

THE DEVIL'S DICTIONARY, *Ambrose Bierce*
Sardonic and irreverent barbs puncturing the pomposities and absurdities of American politics, business, religion, literature, and arts, by the country's greatest satirist in the classic tradition. Epigrammatic as Shaw, piercing as Swift, American as Mark Twain, Will Rogers, and Fred Allen, Bierce will always remain the favorite of a small coterie of enthusiasts, and of writers and speakers whom he supplies with "some of the most gorgeous witticisms of the English language" (H. L. Mencken). Over 1000 entries in alphabetical order. 144pp. 5⅜ x 8. Paperbound $1.00

THE COMPLETE NONSENSE OF EDWARD LEAR.
This is the only complete edition of this master of gentle madness available at a popular price. *A Book of Nonsense, Nonsense Songs, More Nonsense Songs and Stories* in their entirety with all the old favorites that have delighted children and adults for years. The Dong With A Luminous Nose, The Jumblies, The Owl and the Pussycat, and hundreds of other bits of wonderful nonsense. 214 limericks, 3 sets of Nonsense Botany, 5 Nonsense Alphabets, 546 drawings by Lear himself, and much more. 320pp. 5⅜ x 8. Paperbound $1.00

THE WIT AND HUMOR OF OSCAR WILDE, *ed. by Alvin Redman*
Wilde at his most brilliant, in 1000 epigrams exposing weaknesses and hypocrisies of "civilized" society. Divided into 49 categories—sin, wealth, women, America, etc.—to aid writers, speakers. Includes excerpts from his trials, books, plays, criticism. Formerly "The Epigrams of Oscar Wilde." Introduction by Vyvyan Holland, Wilde's only living son. Introductory essay by editor. 260pp. 5⅜ x 8. Paperbound $1.00

A CHILD'S PRIMER OF NATURAL HISTORY, *Oliver Herford*
Scarcely an anthology of whimsy and humor has appeared in the last 50 years without a contribution from Oliver Herford. Yet the works from which these examples are drawn have been almost impossible to obtain! Here at last are Herford's improbable definitions of a menagerie of familiar and weird animals, each verse illustrated by the author's own drawings. 24 drawings in 2 colors; 24 additional drawings. vii + 95pp. 6½ x 6. Paperbound $1.00

THE BROWNIES: THEIR BOOK, *Palmer Cox*
The book that made the Brownies a household word. Generations of readers have enjoyed the antics, predicaments and adventures of these jovial sprites, who emerge from the forest at night to play or to come to the aid of a deserving human. Delightful illustrations by the author decorate nearly every page. 24 short verse tales with 266 illustrations. 155pp. 6⅝ x 9¼.
Paperbound $1.50

THE PRINCIPLES OF PSYCHOLOGY,
William James
The full long-course, unabridged, of one of the great classics of Western literature and science. Wonderfully lucid descriptions of human mental activity, the stream of thought, consciousness, time perception, memory, imagination, emotions, reason, abnormal phenomena, and similar topics. Original contributions are integrated with the work of such men as Berkeley, Binet, Mills, Darwin, Hume, Kant, Royce, Schopenhauer, Spinoza, Locke, Descartes, Galton, Wundt, Lotze, Herbart, Fechner, and scores of others. All contrasting interpretations of mental phenomena are examined in detail—introspective analysis, philosophical interpretation, and experimental research. "A classic," *Journal of Consulting Psychology.* "The main lines are as valid as ever," *Psychoanalytical Quarterly.* "Standard reading . . . a classic of interpretation," *Psychiatric Quarterly.* 94 illustrations. 1408pp. 5⅜ x 8.
Vol. 1 Paperbound $2.50, Vol. 2 Paperbound $2.50,
The set $5.00

VISUAL ILLUSIONS: THEIR CAUSES, CHARACTERISTICS AND APPLICATIONS,
M. Luckiesh
"Seeing is deceiving," asserts the author of this introduction to virtually every type of optical illusion known. The text both describes and explains the principles involved in color illusions, figure-ground, distance illusions, etc. 100 photographs, drawings and diagrams prove how easy it is to fool the sense: circles that aren't round, parallel lines that seem to bend, stationary figures that seem to move as you stare at them — illustration after illustration strains our credulity at what we see. Fascinating book from many points of view, from applications for artists, in camouflage, etc. to the psychology of vision. New introduction by William Ittleson, Dept. of Psychology, Queens College. Index. Bibliography. xxi + 252pp. 5⅜ x 8½.   Paperbound $1.50

FADS AND FALLACIES IN THE NAME OF SCIENCE,
Martin Gardner
This is the standard account of various cults, quack systems, and delusions which have masqueraded as science: hollow earth fanatics. Reich and orgone sex energy, dianetics, Atlantis, multiple moons, Forteanism, flying saucers, medical fallacies like iridiagnosis, zone therapy, etc. A new chapter has been added on Bridey Murphy, psionics, and other recent manifestations in this field. This is a fair, reasoned appraisal of eccentric theory which provides excellent inoculation against cleverly masked nonsense. "Should be read by everyone, scientist and non-scientist alike," R. T. Birge, Prof. Emeritus of Physics, Univ. of California; Former President, American Physical Society. Index. x + 365pp. 5⅜ x 8.   Paperbound $1.85

ILLUSIONS AND DELUSIONS OF THE SUPERNATURAL AND THE OCCULT,
D. H. Rawcliffe
Holds up to rational examination hundreds of persistent delusions including crystal gazing, automatic writing, table turning, mediumistic trances, mental healing, stigmata, lycanthropy, live burial, the Indian Rope Trick, spiritualism, dowsing, telepathy, clairvoyance, ghosts, ESP, etc. The author explains and exposes the mental and physical deceptions involved, making this not only an exposé of supernatural phenomena, but a valuable exposition of characteristic types of abnormal psychology. Originally titled "The Psychology of the Occult." 14 illustrations. Index. 551pp. 5⅜ x 8.   Paperbound $2.25

FAIRY TALE COLLECTIONS, *edited by Andrew Lang*
Andrew Lang's fairy tale collections make up the richest shelf-full of traditional children's stories anywhere available. Lang supervised the translation of stories from all over the world—familiar European tales collected by Grimm, animal stories from Negro Africa, myths of primitive Australia, stories from Russia, Hungary, Iceland, Japan, and many other countries. Lang's selection of translations are unusually high; many authorities consider that the most familiar tales find their best versions in these volumes. All collections are richly decorated and illustrated by H. J. Ford and other artists.

THE BLUE FAIRY BOOK. 37 stories. 138 illustrations. ix + 390pp. 5⅜ x 8½.
Paperbound $1.50

THE GREEN FAIRY BOOK. 42 stories. 100 illustrations. xiii + 366pp. 5⅜ x 8½.
Paperbound $1.50

THE BROWN FAIRY BOOK. 32 stories. 50 illustrations, 8 in color. xii + 350pp. 5⅜ x 8½.
Paperbound $1.50

THE BEST TALES OF HOFFMANN, *edited by E. F. Bleiler*
10 stories by E. T. A. Hoffmann, one of the greatest of all writers of fantasy. The tales include "The Golden Flower Pot," "Automata," "A New Year's Eve Adventure," "Nutcracker and the King of Mice," "Sand-Man," and others. Vigorous characterizations of highly eccentric personalities, remarkably imaginative situations, and intensely fast pacing has made these tales popular all over the world for 150 years. Editor's introduction. 7 drawings by Hoffmann. xxxiii + 419pp. 5⅜ x 8½.
Paperbound $2.00

GHOST AND HORROR STORIES OF AMBROSE BIERCE,
edited by E. F. Bleiler
Morbid, eerie, horrifying tales of possessed poets, shabby aristocrats, revived corpses, and haunted malefactors. Widely acknowledged as the best of their kind between Poe and the moderns, reflecting their author's inner torment and bitter view of life. Includes "Damned Thing," "The Middle Toe of the Right Foot," "The Eyes of the Panther," "Visions of the Night," "Moxon's Master," and over a dozen others. Editor's introduction. xxii + 199pp. 5⅜ x 8½.
Paperbound $1.25

THREE GOTHIC NOVELS, *edited by E. F. Bleiler*
Originators of the still popular Gothic novel form, influential in ushering in early 19th-century Romanticism. Horace Walpole's *Castle of Otranto*, William Beckford's *Vathek*, John Polidori's *The Vampyre*, and a *Fragment* by Lord Byron are enjoyable as exciting reading or as documents in the history of English literature. Editor's introduction. xi + 291pp. 5⅜ x 8½.
Paperbound $2.00

BEST GHOST STORIES OF LEFANU, *edited by E. F. Bleiler*
Though admired by such critics as V. S. Pritchett, Charles Dickens and Henry James, ghost stories by the Irish novelist Joseph Sheridan LeFanu have never become as widely known as his detective fiction. About half of the 16 stories in this collection have never before been available in America. Collection includes "Carmilla" (perhaps the best vampire story ever written), "The Haunted Baronet," "The Fortunes of Sir Robert Ardagh," and the classic "Green Tea." Editor's introduction. 7 contemporary illustrations. Portrait of LeFanu. xii + 467pp. 5⅜ x 8.
Paperbound $2.00

CATALOGUE OF DOVER BOOKS

EASY-TO-DO ENTERTAINMENTS AND DIVERSIONS WITH COINS, CARDS, STRING, PAPER AND MATCHES, *R. M. Abraham*
Over 300 tricks, games and puzzles will provide young readers with absorbing fun. Sections on card games; paper-folding; tricks with coins, matches and pieces of string; games for the agile; toy-making from common household objects; mathematical recreations; and 50 miscellaneous pastimes. Anyone in charge of groups of youngsters, including hard-pressed parents, and in need of suggestions on how to keep children sensibly amused and quietly content will find this book indispensable. Clear, simple text, copious number of delightful line drawings and illustrative diagrams. Originally titled "Winter Nights' Entertainments." Introduction by Lord Baden Powell. 329 illustrations. v + 186pp. 5⅜ x 8½. Paperbound $1.00

AN INTRODUCTION TO CHESS MOVES AND TACTICS SIMPLY EXPLAINED, *Leonard Barden*
Beginner's introduction to the royal game. Names, possible moves of the pieces, definitions of essential terms, how games are won, etc. explained in 30-odd pages. With this background you'll be able to sit right down and play. Balance of book teaches strategy — openings, middle game, typical endgame play, and suggestions for improving your game. A sample game is fully analyzed. True middle-level introduction, teaching you all the essentials without oversimplifying or losing you in a maze of detail. 58 figures. 102pp. 5⅜ x 8½. Paperbound $1.00

LASKER'S MANUAL OF CHESS, *Dr. Emanuel Lasker*
Probably the greatest chess player of modern times, Dr. Emanuel Lasker held the world championship 28 years, independent of passing schools or fashions. This unmatched study of the game, chiefly for intermediate to skilled players, analyzes basic methods, combinations, position play, the aesthetics of chess, dozens of different openings, etc., with constant reference to great modern games. Contains a brilliant exposition of Steinitz's important theories. Introduction by Fred Reinfeld. Tables of Lasker's tournament record. 3 indices. 308 diagrams. 1 photograph. xxx + 349pp. 5⅜ x 8. Paperbound $2.25

COMBINATIONS: THE HEART OF CHESS, *Irving Chernev*
Step-by-step from simple combinations to complex, this book, by a well-known chess writer, shows you the intricacies of pins, counter-pins, knight forks, and smothered mates. Other chapters show alternate lines of play to those taken in actual championship games; boomerang combinations; classic examples of brilliant combination play by Nimzovich, Rubinstein, Tarrasch, Botvinnik, Alekhine and Capablanca. Index. 356 diagrams. ix + 245pp. 5⅜ x 8½. Paperbound $1.85

HOW TO SOLVE CHESS PROBLEMS, *K. S. Howard*
Full of practical suggestions for the fan or the beginner — who knows only the moves of the chessmen. Contains preliminary section and 58 two-move, 46 three-move, and 8 four-move problems composed by 27 outstanding American problem creators in the last 30 years. Explanation of all terms and exhaustive index. "Just what is wanted for the student," Brian Harley. 112 problems, solutions. vi + 171pp. 5⅜ x 8. Paperbound $1.35

SOCIAL THOUGHT FROM LORE TO SCIENCE,
H. E. Barnes and H. Becker
An immense survey of sociological thought and ways of viewing, studying,
planning, and reforming society from earliest times to the present. Includes
thought on society of preliterate peoples, ancient non-Western cultures, and
every great movement in Europe, America, and modern Japan. Analyzes hun-
dreds of great thinkers: Plato, Augustine, Bodin, Vico, Montesquieu, Herder,
Comte, Marx, etc. Weighs the contributions of utopians, sophists, fascists and
communists; economists, jurists, philosophers, ecclesiastics, and every 19th
and 20th century school of scientific sociology, anthropology, and social psy-
chology throughout the world. Combines topical, chronological, and regional
approaches, treating the evolution of social thought as a process rather than
as a series of mere topics. "Impressive accuracy, competence, and discrimina-
tion . . . easily the best single survey," *Nation*. Thoroughly revised, with new
material up to 1960. 2 indexes. Over 2200 bibliographical notes. Three volume
set. Total of 1586pp. 5⅜ x 8.
Vol. 1 Paperbound $2.75, Vol. 2 Paperbound $2.75, Vol. 3 Paperbound $2.50
The set $8.00

A HISTORY OF HISTORICAL WRITING, *Harry Elmer Barnes*
Virtually the only adequate survey of the whole course of historical writing
in a single volume. Surveys developments from the beginnings of historiog-
raphy in the ancient Near East and the Classical World, up through the
Cold War. Covers major historians in detail, shows interrelationship with
cultural background, makes clear individual contributions, evaluates and
estimates importance; also enormously rich upon minor authors and thinkers
who are usually passed over. Packed with scholarship and learning, clear, easily
written. Indispensable to every student of history. Revised and enlarged up
to 1961. Index and bibliography. xv + 442pp. 5⅜ x 8½.   Paperbound $2.50

JOHANN SEBASTIAN BACH, *Philipp Spitta*
The complete and unabridged text of the definitive study of Bach. Written
some 70 years ago, it is still unsurpassed for its coverage of nearly all aspects
of Bach's life and work. There could hardly be a finer non-technical introduc-
tion to Bach's music than the detailed, lucid analyses which Spitta provides
for hundreds of individual pieces. 26 solid pages are devoted to the B minor
mass, for example, and 30 pages to the glorious St. Matthew Passion. This
monumental set also includes a major analysis of the music of the 18th century:
Buxtehude, Pachelbel, etc. "Unchallenged as the last word on one of the
supreme geniuses of music," John Barkham, *Saturday Review Syndicate*. Total
of 1819pp. Heavy cloth binding. 5⅜ x 8.
Two volume set, clothbound $13.50

BEETHOVEN AND HIS NINE SYMPHONIES, *George Grove*
In this modern middle-level classic of musicology Grove not only analyzes all
nine of Beethoven's symphonies very thoroughly in terms of their musical
structure, but also discusses the circumstances under which they were written,
Beethoven's stylistic development, and much other background material. This
is an extremely rich book, yet very easily followed; it is highly recommended
to anyone seriously interested in music. Over 250 musical passages. Index.
viii + 407pp. 5⅜ x 8.   Paperbound $2.00

THREE SCIENCE FICTION NOVELS,
John Taine
Acknowledged by many as the best SF writer of the 1920's, Taine (under the name Eric Temple Bell) was also a Professor of Mathematics of considerable renown. Reprinted here are *The Time Stream*, generally considered Taine's best, *The Greatest Game*, a biological-fiction novel, and *The Purple Sapphire*, involving a supercivilization of the past. Taine's stories tie fantastic narratives to frameworks of original and logical scientific concepts. Speculation is often profound on such questions as the nature of time, concept of entropy, cyclical universes, etc. 4 contemporary illustrations. v + 532pp. 5⅜ x 8⅜.
T1180   Paperbound $2.00

SEVEN SCIENCE FICTION NOVELS,
H. G. Wells
Full unabridged texts of 7 science-fiction novels of the master. Ranging from biology, physics, chemistry, astronomy, to sociology and other studies, Mr. Wells extrapolates whole worlds of strange and intriguing character. "One will have to go far to match this for entertainment, excitement, and sheer pleasure . . ."*New York Times.* Contents: The Time Machine, The Island of Dr. Moreau, The First Men in the Moon, The Invisible Man, The War of the Worlds, The Food of the Gods, In The Days of the Comet. 1015pp. 5⅜ x 8.
T264   Clothbound $5.00

28 SCIENCE FICTION STORIES OF H. G. WELLS.
Two full, unabridged novels, *Men Like Gods* and *Star Begotten*, plus 26 short stories by the master science-fiction writer of all time! Stories of space, time, invention, exploration, futuristic adventure. Partial contents: *The Country of the Blind, In the Abyss, The Crystal Egg, The Man Who Could Work Miracles, A Story of Days to Come, The Empire of the Ants, The Magic Shop, The Valley of the Spiders, A Story of the Stone Age, Under the Knife, Sea Raiders* etc. An indispensable collection for the library of anyone interested in science fiction adventure. 928pp. 5⅜ x 8.   T265   Clothbound $5.00

THREE MARTIAN NOVELS,
Edgar Rice Burroughs
Complete, unabridged reprinting, in one volume, of Thuvia, Maid of Mars; Chessmen of Mars; The Master Mind of Mars. Hours of science-fiction adventure by a modern master storyteller. Reset in large clear type for easy reading. 16 illustrations by J. Allen St. John. vi + 490pp. 5⅜ x 8½.
T39   Paperbound $2.50

AN INTELLECTUAL AND CULTURAL HISTORY OF THE WESTERN WORLD,
Harry Elmer Barnes
Monumental 3-volume survey of intellectual development of Europe from primitive cultures to the present day. Every significant product of human intellect traced through history: art, literature, mathematics, physical sciences, medicine, music, technology, social sciences, religions, jurisprudence, education, etc. Presentation is lucid and specific, analyzing in detail specific discoveries, theories, literary works, and so on. Revised (1965) by recognized scholars in specialized fields under the direction of Prof. Barnes. Revised bibliography. Indexes. 24 illustrations. Total of xxix + 1318pp.
T1275, T1276, T1277   Three volume set, paperbound $7.50

HEAR ME TALKIN' TO YA, *edited by Nat Shapiro and Nat Hentoff*
In their own words, Louis Armstrong, King Oliver, Fletcher Henderson, Bunk Johnson, Bix Beiderbecke, Billy Holiday, Fats Waller, Jelly Roll Morton, Duke Ellington, and many others comment on the origins of jazz in New Orleans and its growth in Chicago's South Side, Kansas City's jam sessions, Depression Harlem, and the modernism of the West Coast schools. Taken from taped conversations, letters, magazine articles, other first-hand sources. Editors' introduction. xvi + 429pp. 5⅜ x 8½.   T1726   Paperbound $2.00

THE JOURNAL OF HENRY D. THOREAU
A 25-year record by the great American observer and critic, as complete a record of a great man's inner life as is anywhere available. Thoreau's Journals served him as raw material for his formal pieces, as a place where he could develop his ideas, as an outlet for his interests in wild life and plants, in writing as an art, in classics of literature, Walt Whitman and other contemporaries, in politics, slavery, individual's relation to the State, etc. The Journals present a portrait of a remarkable man, and are an observant social history. Unabridged republication of 1906 edition, Bradford Torrey and Francis H. Allen, editors. Illustrations. Total of 1888pp. 8⅜ x 12¼.
T312, T313   Two volume set, clothbound $25.00

A SHAKESPEARIAN GRAMMAR, *E. A. Abbott*
Basic reference to Shakespeare and his contemporaries, explaining through thousands of quotations from Shakespeare, Jonson, Beaumont and Fletcher, North's *Plutarch* and other sources the grammatical usage differing from the modern. First published in 1870 and written by a scholar who spent much of his life isolating principles of Elizabethan language, the book is unlikely ever to be superseded. Indexes. xxiv + 511pp. 5⅜ x 8½. T1582 Paperbound $2.75

FOLK-LORE OF SHAKESPEARE, *T. F. Thistelton Dyer*
Classic study, drawing from Shakespeare a large body of references to supernatural beliefs, terminology of falconry and hunting, games and sports, good luck charms, marriage customs, folk medicines, superstitions about plants, animals, birds, argot of the underworld, sexual slang of London, proverbs, drinking customs, weather lore, and much else. From full compilation comes a mirror of the 17th-century popular mind. Index. ix + 526pp. 5⅜ x 8½.
T1614   Paperbound $2.75

THE NEW VARIORUM SHAKESPEARE, *edited by H. H. Furness*
By far the richest editions of the plays ever produced in any country or language. Each volume contains complete text (usually First Folio) of the play, all variants in Quarto and other Folio texts, editorial changes by every major editor to Furness's own time (1900), footnotes to obscure references or language, extensive quotes from literature of Shakespearian criticism, essays on plot sources (often reprinting sources in full), and much more.

HAMLET, *edited by H. H. Furness*
Total of xxvi + 905pp. 5⅜ x 8½.
T1004, T1005   Two volume set, paperbound $5.25

TWELFTH NIGHT, *edited by H. H. Furness*
Index. xxii + 434pp. 5⅜ x 8½.   T1189   Paperbound $2.75

LA BOHEME BY GIACOMO PUCCINI,
translated and introduced by Ellen H. Bleiler
Complete handbook for the operagoer, with everything needed for full enjoy-
ment except the musical score itself. Complete Italian libretto, with new,
modern English line-by-line translation—the only libretto printing all repeats;
biography of Puccini; the librettists; background to the opera, Murger's La
Boheme, etc.; circumstances of composition and performances; plot summary;
and pictorial section of 73 illustrations showing Puccini, famous singers and
performances, etc. Large clear type for easy reading. 124pp. 5⅜ x 8½.
T404   Paperbound $1.00

ANTONIO STRADIVARI: HIS LIFE AND WORK (1644-1737),
W. Henry Hill, Arthur F. Hill, and Alfred E. Hill
Still the only book that really delves into life and art of the incomparable
Italian craftsman, maker of the finest musical instruments in the world today.
The authors, expert violin-makers themselves, discuss Stradivari's ancestry, his
construction and finishing techniques, distinguished characteristics of many
of his instruments and their locations. Included, too, is story of introduction
of his instruments into France, England, first revelation of their supreme
merit, and information on his labels, number of instruments made, prices,
mystery of ingredients of his varnish, tone of pre-1684. Stradivari violin and
changes between 1684 and 1690. An extremely interesting, informative account
for all music lovers, from craftsman to concert-goer. Republication of original
(1902) edition. New introduction by Sydney Beck, Head of Rare Book and
Manuscript Collections, Music Division, New York Public Library. Analytical
index by Rembert Wurlitzer. Appendixes. 68 illustrations. 30 full-page plates.
4 in color. xxvi + 315pp. 5⅜ x 8½.   T425   Paperbound $2.25

MUSICAL AUTOGRAPHS FROM MONTEVERDI TO HINDEMITH,
Emanuel Winternitz
For beauty, for intrinsic interest, for perspective on the composer's personality,
for subtleties of phrasing, shading, emphasis indicated in the autograph but
suppressed in the printed score, the mss. of musical composition are fascinating
documents which repay close study in many different ways. This 2-volume
work reprints facsimiles of mss. by virtually every major composer, and many
minor figures—196 examples in all. A full text points out what can be learned
from mss., analyzes each sample. Index. Bibliography. 18 figures. 196 plates.
Total of 170pp. of text. 7⅞ x 10¾.
T1312, T1313   Two volume set, paperbound $4.00

J. S. BACH,
Albert Schweitzer
One of the few great full-length studies of Bach's life and work, and the
study upon which Schweitzer's renown as a musicologist rests. On first appear-
ance (1911), revolutionized Bach performance. The only writer on Bach to
be musicologist, performing musician, and student of history, theology and
philosophy, Schweitzer contributes particularly full sections on history of Ger-
man Protestant church music, theories on motivic pictorial representations
in vocal music, and practical suggestions for performance. Translated by
Ernest Newman. Indexes. 5 illustrations. 650 musical examples. Total of xix
+ 928pp. 5⅜ x 8½.   T1631, T1632   Two volume set, paperbound $4.50

THE METHODS OF ETHICS, *Henry Sidgwick*
Propounding no organized system of its own, study subjects every major methodological approach to ethics to rigorous, objective analysis. Study discusses and relates ethical thought of Plato, Aristotle, Bentham, Clarke, Butler, Hobbes, Hume, Mill, Spencer, Kant, and dozens of others. Sidgwick retains conclusions from each system which follow from ethical premises, rejecting the faulty. Considered by many in the field to be among the most important treatises on ethical philosophy. Appendix. Index. xlvii + 528pp. 5⅜ x 8½.
T1608   Paperbound $2.50

TEUTONIC MYTHOLOGY, *Jakob Grimm*
A milestone in Western culture; the work which established on a modern basis the study of history of religions and comparative religions. 4-volume work assembles and interprets everything available on religious and folkloristic beliefs of Germanic people (including Scandinavians, Anglo-Saxons, etc.). Assembling material from such sources as Tacitus, surviving Old Norse and Icelandic texts, archeological remains, folktales, surviving superstitions, comparative traditions, linguistic analysis, etc. Grimm explores pagan deities, heroes, folklore of nature, religious practices, and every other area of pagan German belief. To this day, the unrivaled, definitive, exhaustive study. Translated by J. S. Stallybrass from 4th (1883) German edition. Indexes. Total of lxxvii + 1887pp. 5⅜ x 8½.
T1602, T1603, T1604, T1605   Four volume set, paperbound $10.00

THE I CHING, *translated by James Legge*
Called "The Book of Changes" in English, this is one of the Five Classics edited by Confucius, basic and central to Chinese thought. Explains perhaps the most complex system of divination known, founded on the theory that all things happening at any one time have characteristic features which can be isolated and related. Significant in Oriental studies, in history of religions and philosophy, and also to Jungian psychoanalysis and other areas of modern European thought. Index. Appendixes. 6 plates. xxi + 448pp. 5⅜ x 8½.
T1062   Paperbound $2.75

HISTORY OF ANCIENT PHILOSOPHY, *W. Windelband*
One of the clearest, most accurate comprehensive surveys of Greek and Roman philosophy. Discusses ancient philosophy in general, intellectual life in Greece in the 7th and 6th centuries B.C., Thales, Anaximander, Anaximenes, Heraclitus, the Eleatics, Empedocles, Anaxagoras, Leucippus, the Pythagoreans, the Sophists, Socrates, Democritus (20 pages), Plato (50 pages), Aristotle (70 pages), the Peripatetics, Stoics, Epicureans, Sceptics, Neo-platonists, Christian Apologists, etc. 2nd German edition translated by H. E. Cushman. xv + 393pp. 5⅜ x 8.
T357   Paperbound $2.25

THE PALACE OF PLEASURE, *William Painter*
Elizabethan versions of Italian and French novels from *The Decameron*, Cinthio, Straparola, Queen Margaret of Navarre, and other continental sources — the very work that provided Shakespeare and dozens of his contemporaries with many of their plots and sub-plots and, therefore, justly considered one of the most influential books in all English literature. It is also a book that any reader will still enjoy. Total of cviii + 1,224pp.
T1691, T1692, T1693   Three volume set, paperbound $6.75

SHAKESPEARE AS A DRAMATIC ARTIST, *Richard G. Moulton*
Analyses of *Merchant of Venice, Richard III, King Lear, The Tempest,* and
other plays show Shakespeare's skill at integrating story plots, blending light
and serious moods, use of such themes as judgment by appearances, antithesis
of outer and inner life, repeated use of such characters as court fool, and
other important elements. "Only notable book on Shakespeare's handling of
plot . . . one of the most valuable of all books on Shakespeare," Eric Bentley.
Introduction by Eric Bentley. Appendix. Indexes. xviii + 443pp. 5⅜ x 8.
                                          T1546 Paperbound $2.50

THE ENGLISH AND SCOTTISH POPULAR BALLADS, *Francis James Child*
A great work of American scholarship, which established and exhausted a
whole field of literary inquiry. "Child" ballads are those 305 ballads and their
numerous variants preserved orally from medieval, Renaissance and earlier
times. Every known variant (sometimes several dozen) of these ballads known
at the time is given here. Child's commentary traces these ballads' origins,
investigates references in literature, relates them to parallel literary traditions
of other countries. This edition also includes "Professor Child and the Ballad,"
an essay by Prof. Walter Morris Hart. Biographical sketch by G. L. Kittredge.
Appendixes. Total of lxvii + 2694pp. 6½ x 9¼.
             T1409–T1413 Five volume set, Paperbound $13.75

WORLD DRAMA, *edited by B. H. Clark*
The dramatic activity of a score of ages and eras—all in two handy, compact
volumes. More than one-third of this material is unavailable in any other cur-
rent edition! In all, there are 46 plays from the ancient and the modern worlds:
Greece, Rome, Medieval Europe, France, Germany, Italy, England, Russia,
Scandinavia, India, China, Japan, etc.; classic authors such as Aeschylus, Soph-
ocles, Euripides, Aristophanes, Plautus, Marlowe, Jonson, Farquhar, Gold-
smith, Cervantes, Molière, Dumas, Goethe, Schiller, Ibsen. A creative collection
that avoids hackneyed material to include only completely first-rate plays which
are relatively little known or difficult to obtain. "The most comprehensive
collection of important plays from all literature available in English," *Saturday
Review.* Vol. I: Ancient Greece and Rome, China, Japan, Medieval Europe,
England. Vol. II: Modern Europe. Introduction. Reading lists. Total of
1,364pp. 5⅜ x 8.   T57, T59 Two volume set, paperbound $6.00

HISTORY OF PHILOSOPHY, *Julián Marías*
One-volume history of philosophy by a contemporary Spanish philosopher.
Major, perhaps the most important post-war philosophical history. Strong
coverage of recent and still-living philosophers (in many cases the only cover-
age of these figures available at this level) such as Bergson, Jaspers, Buber,
Marcel, Sartre, Whitehead, Russell and Boas; full coverage of Spanish philo-
sophers (particularly the pre-W.W. II School of Madrid) such as Suárez,
Sanz del Río, Santayana, Unamuno and Ortega. Thoroughly organized, lucidly
written for self-study as well as for the classroom. Translated by S. Appelbaum
and C. C. Strowbridge. Bibliography. Index. xix + 505pp. 5⅜ x 8½.
                                          T1739 Paperbound $2.75

THE HUMAN FIGURE IN MOTION, *Eadweard Muybridge*
The largest selection in print of Muybridge's famous high-speed action photos of the human figure in motion. 4789 photographs illustrate 162 different actions: men, women, children—mostly undraped—are shown walking, running, carrying various objects, sitting, lying down, climbing, throwing, arising, and performing over 150 other actions. Some actions are shown in as many as 150 photographs each. All in all there are more than 500 action strips in this enormous volume, series shots taken at shutter speeds of as high as 1/6000th of a second! These are not posed shots, but true stopped motion. They show bone and muscle in situations that the human eye is not fast enough to capture. Earlier, smaller editions of these prints have brought $40 and more on the out-of-print market. "A must for artists," *Art In Focus.* "An unparalleled dictionary of action for all artists," *American Artist.* 390 full-page plates, with 4789 photographs. Printed on heavy glossy stock. Reinforced binding with headbands. xxi + 390pp. 7⅞ x 10⅝.   T204 Clothbound $10.00

THE BOOK OF SIGNS, *Rudolf Koch*
Formerly $20 to $25 on the out-of-print market, now only $1.00 in this unabridged new edition! 493 symbols from ancient manuscripts, medieval cathedrals, coins, catacombs, pottery, etc. Crosses, monograms of Roman emperors, astrological, chemical, botanical, runes, housemarks, and 7 other categories. Invaluable for handicraft workers, illustrators, scholars, etc., this material may be reproduced without permission. 493 illustrations by Fritz Kredel. 104pp. 6½ x 9¼.   T162 Paperbound $1.25

A HANDBOOK OF EARLY ADVERTISING ART, *C. P. Hornung*
The largest collection of copyright-free early advertising art ever compiled. Vol. I contains some 2,000 illustrations of agricultural devices, animals, old automobiles, birds, buildings, Christmas decorations (with 7 Santa Clauses by Nast), allegorical figures, fire engines, horses and vehicles, Indians, portraits, sailing ships, trains, sports, trade cuts—and 30 other categories! Vol. II, devoted to typography, has over 4000 specimens: 600 different Roman, Gothic, Barnum, Old English faces; 630 ornamental type faces; 1115 initials, hundreds of scrolls, flourishes, etc. This third edition is enlarged by 78 additional plates containing all new material. "A remarkable collection," *Printers' Ink.* "A rich contribution to the history of American design," *Graphis.*

Volume 1, Pictorial. Over 2000 illustrations, xiv + 242pp. 9 x 12.
          T122 Clothbound $10.00
Volume 2, Typographical. Over 4000 specimens. vii + 312pp. 9 x 12.
          T123 Clothbound $10.00
          Two volume set, clothbound $20.00

THE STANDARD BOOK OF QUILT MAKING AND COLLECTING, *Marguerite Ickis*
A complete easy-to-follow guide with all the information you need to make beautiful, useful quilts. How to plan, design, cut, sew, appliqué, avoid sewing problems, use rag bag, make borders, tuft, every other aspect. Over 100 traditional quilts shown, including over 40 full-size patterns. At-home hobby for fun, profit. Index. 483 illus. 1 color plate. 287pp. 6¾ x 9½.
          T582 Paperbound $2.25

CATALOGUE OF DOVER BOOKS

DICTIONARY OF AMERICAN PORTRAITS, *edited by Hayward and Blanche Cirker, and the staff of Dover Publications, Inc.*
Reference work and pictorial archive, entirely unique, containing over 4,000 portraits of important Americans who made their impact on American life before approximately 1905. Probably the largest archive of American portraiture ever assembled. The product of many years of investigation and collection, compiled and selected with the assistance of noted authorities in many fields. The work contains a wide representation of figures including Presidents, signers of the Declaration of Independence, diplomats, inventors, businessmen, great men of science and the arts, military figures, Indian leaders, society figures, famous sports figures, pioneers, criminals and their victims, and dozens of other categories. Artist and/or engraver of each portrait supplied where known. List of sources of pictures. Bibliography. Index. 4,045 portraits. xiv + 756pp. 9½ x 12¾.　　　　　　　　　　　　　　　　　T1823 Clothbound $30.00

HEAVENS ON EARTH: UTOPIAN COMMUNITIES IN AMERICA, 1680-1880, *Mark Holloway*
The history of one of young America's strangest adventures: the establishment of strictly regulated communities that strove for a "utopian" existence through adherence to a variety of fascinating and eccentric religious, economic, or social beliefs. The account is entertaining and absorbing as it covers the high intentions, organization, property and buildings, industry and amusements, clothing, beliefs concerning sex, money, and women's rights, reasons for failure, character of the leaders, etc. for virtually every major community that was established: Brook Farm, New Harmony, the Shaker settlements, Oneida, the Fourierist phalanxes, dozens of others. As interesting to the layman as to the historian and the sociologist. Revised (1960) edition. New bibliography. Map. 14 illustrations. xvi + 246pp. 5⅜ x 8½.　　　　　　　　T1593 Paperbound $1.85

INCIDENTS OF TRAVEL IN YUCATAN, *John L. Stephens*
One of the first white men to penetrate interior of Yucatan tells the thrilling story of his discoveries of 44 cities, remains of once-powerful Maya civilization. Compelling text combines narrative power with historical significance as it takes you through heat, dust, storms of Yucatan; native festivals with brutal bull fights; great ruined temples atop man-made mounds. Countless idols, sculptures, tombs, examples of Mayan taste for rich ornamentation, from gateways to personal trinkets, accurately illustrated, discussed in text. Will appeal to those interested in ancient civilizations, and those who like stories of exploration, discovery, adventure. Republication of last (1843) edition. 124 illustrations by English artist, F. Catherwood. Appendix on Mayan architecture, chronology. Total of xxviii + 927pp.
　　　　　　　　　　　　T926, T927 Two volume set, paperbound $4.50

FIGURE DRAWING, *Richard G. Hatton*
One of the few anatomy texts to approach figure drawing from the point of view of the draftsman. Providing wealth of information on anatomy, musculature, etc., but stressing problems of rendering difficult curves and planes of human face and form. Illustrated with 377 figures (with as many as 10 different views of the same subject), showing undraped figures, details of faces, hands, fingers, feet, legs, arms, etc. in dozens of life positions. Index. xi + 350pp. 5⅜ x 8.　　　　　　　　　　　　　　　T1377 Paperbound $2.50

An Introduction to the Geometry of N Dimensions,
D. H. Y. Sommerville
An introduction presupposing no prior knowledge of the field, the only book in English devoted exclusively to higher dimensional geometry. Discusses fundamental ideas of incidence, parallelism, perpendicularity, angles between linear space; enumerative geometry; analytical geometry from projective and metric points of view; polytopes; elementary ideas in analysis situs; content of hyper-spacial figures. Bibliography. Index. 60 diagrams. 196pp. 5⅜ x 8.
Paperbound $1.50

Elementary Concepts of Topology, *P. Alexandroff*
First English translation of the famous brief introduction to topology for the beginner or for the mathematician not undertaking extensive study. This unusually useful intuitive approach deals primarily with the concepts of complex, cycle, and homology, and is wholly consistent with current investigations. Ranges from basic concepts of set-theoretic topology to the concept of Betti groups. "Glowing example of harmony between intuition and thought," David Hilbert. Translated by A. E. Farley. Introduction by D. Hilbert. Index. 25 figures. 73pp. 5⅜ x 8.
Paperbound $1.00

Elements of Non-Euclidean Geometry,
D. M. Y. Sommerville
Unique in proceeding step-by-step, in the manner of traditional geometry. Enables the student with only a good knowledge of high school algebra and geometry to grasp elementary hyperbolic, elliptic, analytic non-Euclidean geometries; space curvature and its philosophical implications; theory of radical axes; homothetic centres and systems of circles; parataxy and parallelism; absolute measure; Gauss' proof of the defect area theorem; geodesic representation; much more, all with exceptional clarity. 126 problems at chapter endings provide progressive practice and familiarity. 133 figures. Index. xvi + 274pp. 5⅜ x 8.
Paperbound $2.00

Introduction to the Theory of Numbers, *L. E. Dickson*
Thorough, comprehensive approach with adequate coverage of classical literature, an introductory volume beginners can follow. Chapters on divisibility, congruences, quadratic residues & reciprocity. Diophantine equations, etc. Full treatment of binary quadratic forms without usual restriction to integral coefficients. Covers infinitude of primes, least residues. Fermat's theorem. Euler's phi function, Legendre's symbol, Gauss's lemma, automorphs, reduced forms, recent theorems of Thue & Siegel, many more. Much material not readily available elsewhere. 239 problems. Index. I figure. viii + 183pp. 5⅜ x 8.
Paperbound $1.75

Mathematical Tables and Formulas,
compiled by Robert D. Carmichael and Edwin R. Smith
Valuable collection for students, etc. Contains all tables necessary in college algebra and trigonometry, such as five-place common logarithms, logarithmic sines and tangents of small angles, logarithmic trigonometric functions, natural trigonometric functions, four-place antilogarithms, tables for changing from sexagesimal to circular and from circular to sexagesimal measure of angles, etc. Also many tables and formulas not ordinarily accessible, including powers, roots, and reciprocals, exponential and hyperbolic functions, ten-place logarithms of prime numbers, and formulas and theorems from analytical and elementary geometry and from calculus. Explanatory introduction. viii + 269pp. 5⅜ x 8½.
Paperbound $1.25

A Source Book in Mathematics,
D. E. Smith
Great discoveries in math, from Renaissance to end of 19th century, in English translation. Read announcements by Dedekind, Gauss, Delamain, Pascal, Fermat, Newton, Abel, Lobachevsky, Bolyai, Riemann, De Moivre, Legendre, Laplace, others of discoveries about imaginary numbers, number congruence, slide rule, equations, symbolism, cubic algebraic equations, non-Euclidean forms of geometry, calculus, function theory, quaternions, etc. Succinct selections from 125 different treatises, articles, most unavailable elsewhere in English. Each article preceded by biographical introduction. Vol. I: Fields of Number, Algebra. Index. 32 illus. 338pp. 5⅜ x 8. Vol. II: Fields of Geometry, Probability, Calculus, Functions, Quaternions. 83 illus. 432pp. 5⅜ x 8.
Vol. 1 Paperbound $2.00, Vol. 2 Paperbound $2.00,
The set $4.00

Foundations of Physics,
R. B. Lindsay & H. Margenau
Excellent bridge between semi-popular works & technical treatises. A discussion of methods of physical description, construction of theory; valuable for physicist with elementary calculus who is interested in ideas that give meaning to data, tools of modern physics. Contents include symbolism; mathematical equations; space & time foundations of mechanics; probability; physics & continua; electron theory; special & general relativity; quantum mechanics; causality. "Thorough and yet not overdetailed. Unreservedly recommended," *Nature* (London). Unabridged, corrected edition. List of recommended readings. 35 illustrations. xi + 537pp. 5⅜ x 8.   Paperbound $3.00

Fundamental Formulas of Physics,
ed. by D. H. Menzel
High useful, full, inexpensive reference and study text, ranging from simple to highly sophisticated operations. Mathematics integrated into text—each chapter stands as short textbook of field represented. Vol. 1: Statistics, Physical Constants, Special Theory of Relativity, Hydrodynamics, Aerodynamics, Boundary Value Problems in Math, Physics, Viscosity, Electromagnetic Theory, etc. Vol. 2: Sound, Acoustics, Geometrical Optics, Electron Optics, High-Energy Phenomena, Magnetism, Biophysics, much more. Index. Total of 800pp. 5⅜ x 8.
Vol. 1 Paperbound $2.25, Vol. 2 Paperbound $2.25,
The set $4.50

Theoretical Physics,
A. S. Kompaneyets
One of the very few thorough studies of the subject in this price range. Provides advanced students with a comprehensive theoretical background. Especially strong on recent experimentation and developments in quantum theory. Contents: Mechanics (Generalized Coordinates, Lagrange's Equation, Collision of Particles, etc.), Electrodynamics (Vector Analysis, Maxwell's equations, Transmission of Signals, Theory of Relativity, etc.), Quantum Mechanics (the Inadequacy of Classical Mechanics, the Wave Equation, Motion in a Central Field, Quantum Theory of Radiation, Quantum Theories of Dispersion and Scattering, etc.), and Statistical Physics (Equilibrium Distribution of Molecules in an Ideal Gas, Boltzmann Statistics, Bose and Fermi Distribution. Thermodynamic Quantities, etc.). Revised to 1961. Translated by George Yankovsky, authorized by Kompaneyets. 137 exercises. 56 figures. 529pp. 5⅜ x 8½.
Paperbound $2.50

THE WONDERFUL WIZARD OF OZ, *L. F. Baum*
All the original W. W. Denslow illustrations in full color—as much a part of
"The Wizard" as Tenniel's drawings are of "Alice in Wonderland." "The
Wizard" is still America's best-loved fairy tale, in which, as the author expresses
it, "The wonderment and joy are retained and the heartaches and nightmares
left out." Now today's young readers can enjoy every word and wonderful pic-
ture of the original book. New introduction by Martin Gardner. A Baum
bibliography. 23 full-page color plates. viii + 268pp. 5⅜ x 8.
                                                T691   Paperbound $1.75

THE MARVELOUS LAND OF OZ, *L. F. Baum*
This is the equally enchanting sequel to the "Wizard," continuing the adven-
tures of the Scarecrow and the Tin Woodman. The hero this time is a little
boy named Tip, and all the delightful Oz magic is still present. This is the
Oz book with the Animated Saw-Horse, the Woggle-Bug, and Jack Pumpkin-
head. All the original John R. Neill illustrations, 10 in full color. 287pp.
5⅜ x 8.   T692   Paperbound $1.50

ALICE'S ADVENTURES UNDER GROUND, *Lewis Carroll*
The original *Alice in Wonderland*, hand-lettered and illustrated by Carroll
himself, and originally presented as a Christmas gift to a child-friend. Adults
as well as children will enjoy this charming volume, reproduced faithfully
in this Dover edition. While the story is essentially the same, there are slight
changes, and Carroll's spritely drawings present an intriguing alternative to
the famous Tenniel illustrations. One of the most popular books in Dover's
catalogue. Introduction by Martin Gardner. 38 illustrations. 128pp. 5⅜ x 8½.
                                                T1482   Paperbound $1.00

THE NURSERY "ALICE," *Lewis Carroll*
While most of us consider *Alice in Wonderland* a story for children of all
ages, Carroll himself felt it was beyond younger children. He therefore pro-
vided this simplified version, illustrated with the famous Tenniel drawings
enlarged and colored in delicate tints, for children aged "from Nought to
Five." Dover's edition of this now rare classic is a faithful copy of the 1889
printing, including 20 illustrations by Tenniel, and front and back covers
reproduced in full color. Introduction by Martin Gardner. xxiii + 67pp.
6⅛ x 9¼.   T1610   Paperbound $1.75

THE STORY OF KING ARTHUR AND HIS KNIGHTS, *Howard Pyle*
A fast-paced, exciting retelling of the best known Arthurian legends for young
readers by one of America's best story tellers and illustrators. The sword
Excalibur, wooing of Guinevere, Merlin and his downfall, adventures of Sir
Pellias and Gawaine, and others. The pen and ink illustrations are vividly
imagined and wonderfully drawn. 41 illustrations. xviii + 313pp. 6⅛ x 9¼.
                                                T1445   Paperbound $1.75

Prices subject to change without notice.

Available at your book dealer or write for free catalogue to Dept. Adsci,
Dover Publications, Inc., 180 Varick St., N.Y., N.Y. 10014. Dover publishes more
than 150 books each year on science, elementary and advanced mathematics,
biology, music, art, literary history, social sciences and other areas.